English for Nurses

Edited by

Nitin Bhatnagar

Pearson

Editor—Acquisitions: Prasun Chatterjee
Associate Editor—Production: Amrita Naskar

ISBN 978-81-317-6962-1

First Impression, 2012
Second Impression, 2018

Published by Pearson India Education Services Pvt. Ltd, CIN: U72200TN2005PTC057128.

Head Office:15th Floor, Tower-B, World Trade Tower, Plot No. 1, Block-C, Sector 16,
Noida 201 301, Uttar Pradesh, India.
Registered Office: 4th Floor, Software Block, Elnet Software City, TS-140, Block 2 & 9,
Rajiv Gandhi Salai, Taramani, Chennai 600 113, Tamil Nadu, India.
Fax: 080-30461003, Phone: 080-30461060
Website: in.pearson.com, Email: companysecretary.india@pearson.com

Compositor: Sunrise Media Solutions
Printed in India at India Binding House, Noida.

Permissions and Acknowledgements

Chapter 1, 'Edith Cavell: And Bravely Fought the Nurse': Extracted from http://www.stainesparish.org/impactoct2009.pdf, accessed on 7 March 2012.

Chapter 2, 'The Story of a British Nurse': Extracted from Margaret Ledger, 'A Queen Alexandra's Nurse in India', Stockport Libraries, http://www.bbc.co.uk/ww2peopleswar/stories/66/a2838666.shtml, accessed on 7 March 2012.

Chapter 3, 'A Doctor for All Seasons': Reprinted with permission from www.thehindu. com/mag/2007/08/05/.../2007080550150500.htm, accessed on 8 December 2011.

Chapter 4, 'Aarohi: Himalayan Care': Extracted from http://aarohi.org/reach_us.php, accessed on 7 March 2012.

Chapter 5, 'Communication in Healthcare: The Perspective of a Nurse': Reprinted with permission from Philip Burnard and Paul Gill, *Culture, Communication and Nursing*, Pearson Education, © Pearson Education Ltd, United Kingdom.

Chapter 6, 'Private and Public Partnership in Healthcare': Extracted from *The Lancet*, Vol. 372, Issue 9642, Pages 878–879, 13 September 2008, © Elsevier, reprinted with permission from CCC.

Chapter 7, 'Managing Pain': Reprinted with permission from Philip Burnard and Paul Gill, *Culture, Communication and Nursing*, Pearson Education, © Pearson Education Ltd, United Kingdom.

Chapter 8, 'Stress in Nursing': Extracted from P. P. Kane, 'Stress Causing Psychosomatic Illness among Nurses', *Indian Journal of Occupational and Environmental Medicine* 2009, 13:28–32.

Chapter 9, 'The Quiet Soldiers of Compassion': Reprinted with permission from *Tehelka*, Vol 5, Issue 33, 23 August 2008.

Chapter 10, 'The Story of a Caribbean Nurse': Extracted from http://www.bbc.co.uk/ww2peopleswar/stories/31/a4167731.shtml, accessed on 7 March 2012.

Contents

Preface *vii*
About the Editor *ix*

1 Edith Cavell: And Bravely Fought the Nurse 1
2 The Story of a British Nurse 7
3 A Doctor for All Seasons 14
4 Aarohi: Himalayan Care 19
5 Communication in Healthcare: The Perspective of a Nurse 23
6 Private and Public Partnership in Healthcare 28
7 Managing Pain 36
8 Stress in Nursing 40
9 The Quiet Soldiers of Compassion 48
10 The Story of a Caribbean Nurse 57
Appendix 1: Group Discussion 63
Appendix 2: Written Communication 79
Appendix 3: Report Writing 103

Preface

This volume has been created taking note of the requirements of students of nursing in terms of communication and soft skills in English. In the emerging scenario of increasing demand for Indian nurses abroad, the ability to communicate effectively has become the prime requirement for the practising nurses. The need for professional nurses with fluency in spoken and written English is increasing in India as well due to several private hospital chains entering to serve in this profession. *English for Nurses* takes into account these changes and imparts the entire range of skills required to be successful in the profession.

Unlike other books which enter the technical details of the profession, the aim of this book is to widen the range of topics related to medical and nursing. The chapters in *English for Nurses*, related to the field of healthcare, provide practice in all the four aspects of reading, writing, listening and speaking skills. At the end of each chapter, there are exercises linked to the reading passages; these make the students proficient in their writing abilities.

Being a part of the profession of nursing not only requires knowledge of healthcare practices but also moral and ethical values to help mitigate pain and effectively assist patients. The themes, based on these pertinent aspects of healthcare, have been chosen to inculcate these values in the users of this book. So, a complete package required for the nurses to be confident about their communication skills and the perspective required for nursing is presented in this book. I hope that it will help the students and nurses to meet the challenges in their profession.

Nitin Bhatnagar

About the Editor

Nitin Bhatnagar is Professor of English, GLA University, Mathura. He has taught English language skills, professional communication and English literature at various levels for over two and a half decades now. His expertise lies in training learners for oral professional communication using Computer Aided Language Learning (CALL). He has also been guiding students for competitive examinations and preparing them for placements in companies. He has been associated with many reputed universities and institutes as a visiting faculty and has delivered expert lectures on various aspects of professional communication. He did his Ph.D. from Devi Ahilya University, Indore, and is currently supervising many scholars for their doctoral research. He has written many research papers, which have been published in various national and international journals.

1

Edith Cavell: And Bravely Fought the Nurse

Edith Cavell was born to a priest's family in Norwich. Marton Eva Luckes trained her as a nurse in Brussels. L'École Belge d'Infirmières Diplômées on the Rue de la Culture in Brussels was the place where she became a matron. By 1910, Miss Cavell 'felt that the profession of nursing had gained sufficient foothold in Belgium to **warrant** the publishing of a professional journal', and therefore launched the nursing journal, L'infirmière. A year later, she was a training nurse for three hospitals, 24 schools and 13 kindergartens in Belgium.

When World War I broke out, she was visiting her widowed mother in Norfolk. She returned to Brussels where her clinic and nursing school were taken over by the Red Cross.

In the autumn of 1914, after the German occupation of Brussels, Cavell began sheltering British soldiers and **funnelling** them out of occupied Belgium to neutral Holland. In the following months, an underground organization developed, allowing her to guide some 200 Allied soldiers to safety, which placed Cavell in violation of German military law. German authorities became increasingly suspicious of the nurse's actions, which were reinforced by Cavell's own disregard and **outspokenness**.

She was arrested on 3 August 1915 and charged with harbouring Allied soldiers. She was held in St Gilles prison for 10 weeks, the last two in solitary **confinement** and **court-martialed.**

The British government said they could do nothing to help her. Sir Horace Rowland of the Foreign Office said, 'I am afraid that it is likely to go hard with Miss Cavell; I am afraid we are powerless'. The sentiment was echoed by Lord Robert Cecil, Under-Secretary for Foreign Affairs. 'Any representation by us', he advised, 'will do her more harm than good'. The United States, which had not yet joined the war, did not agree. Hugh S. Gibson, First Secretary of the American legation at Brussels, made clear to the German government that executing Cavell would further harm their nation's already damaged reputation. Later, he wrote:

> We reminded him (Baron von der Lancken) of the burning of Louvain and the sinking of the Lusitania and told him that this murder would stir all civilized countries with horror and disgust. Count Harrach broke in at this with the remark that he would rather see Miss Cavell shot than have harm come to one of the humblest German soldiers, and his only regret was that they had not three or four English old women to shoot.

The German civil governor, Baron von der Lancken, is known to have stated that Cavell should be pardoned because of her complete honesty and because she had helped save so many lives, German as well as Allied. However, the German military acted quickly to execute Cavell to deny higher authorities the opportunity to consider **clemency**.

She was not arrested for **espionage** as many were led to believe, but for **treason**. Of the 27 put on trial, Cavell and four others were condemned to death, among them Philippe Baucq, an architect in his thirties who was also **instrumental** in the escapes.

When in custody, Cavell was asked questions in French, with **transcripts** made in German. This process gave the **inquisitor** the opportunity to misinterpret her answers. Although she may have been misrepresented, she made no attempt to defend herself. Cavell was provided with a defender approved by the German military governor. A previous defender, who was chosen for Cavell by her assistant, Elizabeth Wilkins, was ultimately denied by the governor.

The night before her execution, she told the Reverend Stirling Gahan, the Anglican chaplain who had been allowed to see her and to give her Holy Communion, 'Patriotism is not enough, I must have no hatred or bitterness towards anyone.' These words are inscribed on her statue in St Martin's Place, near Trafalgar Square in London. Her final words to the German Lutheran prison chaplain, Paul Le Seur, were recorded as, 'Ask Father Gahan to tell my loved ones later on that my soul, as I believe, is safe, and that I am glad to die for my country.'

Despite efforts by American minister Brand Whitlock and the Marquis de Villalobar, the Spanish minister to Belgium, on Cavell's behalf, on 11 October, Baron Von Der Lancken allowed the execution to proceed. Sixteen men, composed of two firing squads, carried out her sentence along with four Belgian men at Tir Nationalshooting range in Schaerbeek, at 6 am on 12 October 1915. There are conflicting reports of the details of Cavell's execution. However, according to the eyewitness account of the Reverend Le Seur, who attended Cavell in her final hours, eight soldiers fired at Cavell while the other eight executed Philippe Baucq.

There is also a dispute over the sentencing imposed under German Military Code. Supposedly, the death penalty equivalent to the offence committed by Cavell was not officially declared until a few hours after her death.

With instructions from the Spanish minister, Belgian women immediately buried her body next to St. Gilles Prison. After the war, her body was taken back to Britain for a memorial service at Westminster Abbey and again transferred to Norwich, to finally be laid to rest at Life's Green.

Vocabulary

1. **Warrant:** Make it necessary
2. **Funnelling:** The expression generally refers to the passage of things through a conical channel. Here, it suggests that Edith was the channel through whom British soldiers found a way to neutral Holland.
3. **Outspokenness:** The nature of being frank and honest with one's opinion
4. **Confinement:** Imprisonment, a state of restriction
5. **Court-martialed:** Trial in a military court where the accused is charged with treason or acting against the military code of conduct
6. **Espionage:** Spy missions in foreign countries
7. **Treason:** Acting against the interests of the state under whose rule one is placed
8. **Instrumental:** Being the key to a certain event
9. **Inquisitor:** A kind of character who participates in witch-hunting trying to extract information of people's secret crimes or sins. In the middle ages, Spain had catholic inquistors whose responsibility was to compell individuals to confess their moments of untruth and interaction with the Devil.
10. **Transcripts:** Records of oral communication in an official atmosphere

Reading Comprehension

On the basis of the above passage, answer the following questions:

1. Who was the teacher of Florence Nightingale and Edith Cavell?
2. Name the journal that Edith Cavell started. What was the language in which it was published?
3. What happened to her clinic and nursing school after World War I broke out?
4. What did Edith do to earn the ire of the Germans? How far was their dissapproval justified?
5. What was the charge under which Edith was arrested? From a purely legal point of view, was it justifiable?
6. Explain Edith's comment: 'Patriotism is not enough, I must have no hatred or bitterness towards anyone.'
7. Describe the way in which Edith was executed. Do you think it was unecessarily cruel?

Language

Read the following sentences:

a) 'Edith Cavell was[1] born to a priest's family in Norwich. Marton Eva Luckes trained[2] her as a nurse in Brussels'.

b) 'A year later, she was[3] a training nurse for three hospitals, 24 schools and 13 kindergartens in Belgium'.
c) 'When World War I broke out, she was visiting[4] her widowed mother in Norfolk'.

All these sentences deal with events that refer to situations in the past. 1, 2 *and* 3 are ***simple past tenses***, *whereas* 4 *refers to the* **past continuous tense**.

Exercise

Work with your instructor to arrive at a definition of the past continuous tense. (Hint: Edith's visit to her widowed mother coincided with the break of the war. So, one event was being completed as another had already occurred).

Remember that we use the simple past tense accompanying adverbs or phrases of time. Read the following sentence to pick out the phrase of time.

Last year, Christina **used to** manage the High Dependence Unit of the gastrointestinal surgery department.

In the above sentence, **Last year** is a phrase of time. The expression **used to** combines with the verb **manage** to convey the sense of an action which took place regularly at a certain point of time and has been discontinued.

Correct the following sentences:

1. Sumithra was the incharge of the intensive care unit since last year.
2. Nurses from Kollam administer pulse polio vaccines in the spring camp that take place last year.
3. Last month, nurses from our unit apply for positions in the United Kingdom.
4. The doctor is angry with the nurse who is misbehave with a patient.
5. When my son is recovering from burns, it is a nurse from Calicut who help him the most.
6. While I administer fluids to the patient, he collapse and become unconscious.
7. Throughout the night, the old woman gasp for breath and the doctor is late to come.
8. We were knowing that the patient will take time to recover.
9. Se is a good nurse in the pediatrics department. She take good care of babies there.
10. The nurse call the doctor as the patient do not respond to ventilator.

Functions

Read the following conversation between two nursing assistants:

Roselyn: Maria, can you check the patient in Room 101, **please**.

Maria: Sure. **What's up**?

Roselyn: I think her IV fluid inflow has stopped. It **needs to be** restarted. You **might need to** create a new channel as well.

Maria: **No problem**. I'll be there in a minute.

Roselyn: Thanks a ton, Maria.

Now check the words in bold. These words are functions that facilitate conversation making it lively. These are language units linked to specific communicative contexts. The more you talk, the more you are adept at handling such functions. The functions like 'What's up?' are phrases that belong to a longer sentence structure. For instance, 'What is up with X?' has been shortened to 'What's up?' These contractions are peculiar to speech communication. Qualifiers like 'you might need' are ways of imparting instructions. The expression 'no problem' expresses agreement and is a part of the language structure, it is not a problem. Learning these words and expressions are essential ways of learning communicative grammar.

Imagine another problem and another way of trouble shooting.

Here are some cues. Fill in the blanks using your own words.

Roselyn: Hi Maria! Can you please check __________ in Room 105?

Maria: Hi! _______, but what is the ____________?

Roselyn: The doctor is dressing the patient, and she has run out of _____ _________.

Maria: Right. I'll get some from our ______ and write a prescription for it.

Roselyn: _________!

Pronunciation: '-*ed*' ending

While the –*ed* ending in written communication forms the past tense of regular verbs, in spoken communication, the –*ed* ending can have different pronunciations. It can sound like [t] (as in *stopped*); [d] (as in *saved*); or [Id] (as in *loaded*)

Exercise

Read the words aloud and get your –*ed* sound right!

- stopped
- ended
- filled
- wounded
- cried
- hunted
- injected
- dressed

Writing

Write a paragraph about a nurse's day in the hospital. You are privy to a diary she keeps. Read the diary to formulate your paragraph.

Remember that a paragraph is about **one main idea**. The sentence expressing that idea is called a **topic sentence**. In a paragraph, one must avoid writing any sentence that exceeds the scope of the topic sentence.

Here are some pointers from which the topic sentence is expected to emerge.

a) I reached the ward at half-past eight.
b) Sheela was in a bad mood. A patient had passed away in the night.
c) The handover note was quite a mess. A number of tests were due. Someone who was advised Magnex hadn't got it from the dispensary.
d) Had lunch with Rose. She is getting married next month.
e) There were two new patients from the theatre. Both were on ventilation.
f) Didn't get time for tea in the evening.

Topic sentence: It was an extremely busy day.

Concluding sentence: A nurse in a government hospital has a tough time.

Remember: That the topic sentence and the concluding sentence match in terms of purpose and register. Do not try to introduce a new strand as you close your discussion.

2 The Story of a British Nurse

Margaret Ledger

I left Lady Manners' School in Bakewell, Derbyshire in 1939. Europe was beginning to fall under the control of Hitler. Germany had become very powerful, and it was becoming obvious that England would be at war against Germany. I was 18 years of age, so I knew I had to do something useful for the Country. I decided to become a nurse. I commenced my nurse training at the Chesterfield and North Derbyshire Royal Hospital on the 18th September 1939. War had been declared. The training was to take four years—from September 1939 to October 1943.

During my nurse training days, we had lectures from the doctors and the nurse tutor. We worked hard on the wards and departments including the Operating Theatre. There were air raids at night-time. The wards and departments were all blacked-out, and when the air raid sirens sounded, we covered the patients' heads with little pillows. The training was hard, but I thoroughly enjoyed myself. It was so interesting. At the end of my first year, I sat for my preliminary examination. After three years training I sat my State Registered Examination, I passed and was given the title 'State Registered Nurse' (i.e., SRN). I became a Staff Nurse. I was allowed to check drugs and to be in charge of a ward.

At the end of my four years' training, I joined the Queen Alexandra's Imperial Nursing Service. The Army, the Navy and the Royal Air Force were asking for trained nurses to look after their wounded men to serve in England and Overseas wherever the Forces were stationed. The Queen Alexandra's Nurses were serving with the Army in India and other places of the Empire before the War. This Service had a long history developing from the Army Nursing Service established by Florence Nightingale in the Crimea. Therefore it was a very well established Nursing Service. So were those serving the Navy and the Air Force?

On applying for the Q.A.I.M.N.S, I was interviewed at York and then returned to Chesterfield Hospital to await orders. After about one month, I was informed that I had to report to the Examination School in Oxford and to live in Lincoln College. When I arrived in Oxford, I purchased my uniform—both indoor and outdoor. I was given a full medical examination and various **inoculations**. The typhoid injection had nasty side effects. At Oxford, there were several Nursing Sisters and a well-established Military Hospital in the Examination School. After six weeks, a number of us Nursing Sisters were sent on embarkation leave (I think it was for two weeks). We were now in a grey and scarlet uniform—a very smart outfit. It was all very exciting for me and very upsetting for my parents. However it was war and we were eager to help.

On our return to Oxford, we obtained our tropical uniform and eventually were given orders to be prepared to move on. The orders came at midnight in December 1943, and we all moved from Oxford Station at about 2am. The huge long train was all blacked-out. We Nursing Sisters travelled First Class. It seemed a never-ending journey. It was, because we eventually arrived in Scotland, at Greenock on the Cylde. There were several large ships on the Cylde. Our ship was to be the 'Stratheden'. There were **aircraft carriers**, battleships, **corvettes** and two large ships. One was ours the 'Stratheden'. We all boarded a light ship, which took us to the 'Stratheden'. We stayed on board for one day; we did boat drill and were given other instructions. Finally, we set sail during the night. All ships were blacked-out. It seems but a dream. We all experienced sea sickness; however, we recovered. After several days at sea, we finally entered Algiers harbour on Christmas Eve 1943 and anchored there until **Boxing Day**. When all the convoy then set sail again out into the Mediterranean Sea, we could see only water for miles.

Eventually, we arrived at Port Said. The escort ships disappeared, probably to escort other ships. The personnel from the two troop ships disembarked and were sent to various places. The Nursing Sisters on the 'Stratheden' were transported to a transit camp. This was a tented place. After about a week, we were told to pack our bags, and we were transported by a large truck to Port Suez, where we embarked on a ship 'The Sythia'. It had been damaged but repaired. On board were New Zealanders, Maoris and Australians. The troops had been prisoners in Crete and had also fought in the North African Campaign. We eventually arrived in Bombay, India. The Nursing Sisters, Doctors and other English personnel **disembarked**, leaving the New Zealanders, Maoris and Australians to sail on to their respective country.

At Bombay Station, where we assembled, we were given further instructions by officers, who were awaiting our arrival. We were all dispensed into various trains. I was posted with other Nursing Sisters to Secunderabad. It is in Hyderabad Province. Eventually, we arrived at our destination, after travelling several days in the train. We were tired and it was very hot and humid.

The next day we commenced our nursing duties. I was posted to the Operating Theatre. We **sterilized** our instruments in large fish kettles, and the work consisted of casualties transported from the front line in Burma. The casualties were British, Indian, African and other personnel brought to Base Hospitals by train. Some had been shipped by hospital ships to Madras, then conveyed by train to various military hospitals. Some had travelled for days in the heat of India and were very weary. They had dysentery and malaria and other topical diseases, as well as their severe wounds. The Operating Theatre staff worked from 7.00am or before that time until 12 midday. No patient was anaesthetized during the heat of the afternoon, it was too hot. Therefore, work commenced again at 5.00pm or 6.00pm. There was no air conditioning or fans in the Operating Theatre. We were all sweating and it was very hot with masks over our faces. However, we survived and progressed with our work.

After nine months in Secunderabad, I was posted to a jungle hospital in Mysore Jungle, many miles away from Secunderabad. I travelled alone on the train to Bangalore. There were other travellers on the train, mostly natives of India and some British troops, but I was the only Nursing Sister. I was locked in my small compartment, and at every station we stopped, an officer came to check that I was safe. There were many incidents on the trains, chiefly stealing. However, I eventually arrived in Bangalore Station and was conveyed to the British Military Hospital by an officer, who had been awaiting my arrival.

At Bangalore Military Hospital, I met two other Nursing Sisters, who had been posted to the Jungle Hospital. We awaited further instructions from G.H.Q. Delhi. During this time, we worked in the British Military Hospital in Bangalore. The patients were similar to the casualties in Secunderabad. There were Italian prisoners of war, who were captured in North Africa, who were employed on general duties. They were very polite but enjoyed hiding away from work. One day, three of them had disappeared, and I went to search for them because we were short of staff. They were sitting outside the Quartermaster's Stores. I told them to come back to the ward. In a chorus of three voices, they replied 'Madam, we do not make war, we make love'.

Eventually Eileen, Margaret and myself received orders to proceed to Gudalur in Mysore Jungle. We boarded a train to Mysore, and we were met by the Commanding Officer, Major Bathgate, who had brought adequate transport to enable our tin trucks and other luggage to be conveyed with ourselves to the Jungle Hospital, which was to be our home. It was a memorable time; we stayed in Gudalur for five months. It was a small hospital, 105 bedded in tents, Indian, Gurkha and English patients. The two Medical Officers were Major Bathgate and Capt. Henry Oaks. The Nursing Sisters were Eileen Bowman, Margaret David and Margaret Ledger. The Nursing Orderlies were mainly British with a few Indian and Gurkha. We were kept busy with various **tropical diseases**; accidents were frequent because there were many troops in the jungle, all preparing to go to Burma. This was 1944 and the Burma Campaign was in full activity. Many of the men were ill with various complaints; therefore, the hospital was always busy. The three of us enjoyed our daily tasks. We did not have days off, but we kept going and enjoyed the experience. We were all very happy in this jungle.

Everyone in training was taught to work in rough conditions and to be self-supporting. I learnt to drive a Jeep and ride a large cavalry horse. We were supposed to have lessons in shooting a gun, but it did not materialize. Our outfit in the jungle was bush jacket and slacks, large boots and socks. It was a high malarial area; therefore, we had to take mepacrine tablets daily. It was an antimalarial treatment. Our skin became very yellow, but we never developed malaria, in fact we never contracted any of the tropical diseases. Our lighting was by hurricane oil lamps.

The bath tubs were small canvas ones. The three of us slept together in a medium sized tent, we each had our own **camp bed**. There was no running water; it was brought to us by the Batman, Indian or Gurkha, in a large tin bucket. Three buckets would arrive and the water was very hot as there was no cold water. We were on restricted amounts of water. Our toilets were small pots elevated on a stand and emptied by the 'sweeper'.

We lived with the wild animals; there were many—monkeys, elephants, wild boar, snakes and tigers, but we never saw any. The soldiers on exercise in the jungle met many wild animals. Bamboo and other tall trees surrounded us. There were large snakes around, but we never saw any. Scorpions were an every day appearance. There were white ants, which would build a huge mound over night. It was incredible how fast they worked. There were millions of them, they would sting our feet when they managed to invade our bedding and shoes. We slept beneath mosquito nets. A life that will never be forgotten, and I frequently recall the wild life that lived in the jungle. The birds and white ants were plentiful. The monkeys gave so many amusing moments with their **inquisitive** ways.

We spent Christmas in our jungle home, which was very interesting. Traditional Christmas puddings were served, but we ate wild boar. In January 1945, orders came from G.H.Q. Delhi that the Hospital was to close, and the three Nursing Sisters were posted to the British Military Hospital in Wellington in the Nilgiri Hills.

It was a great relief from the intense heat in the jungle. The effects of our primitive life were beginning to show; however, it was pleasing to be able to sleep without the mosquito nets and to have a good hot bath without fat floating on the top, as it had done in our jungle home. The Military Hospital in Wellington, South India, was a peacetime hospital, a hill station and our quarters were lovely and **cozy**. We had fires in our sitting rooms and we burnt eucalyptus leaves on the room fires. We were given fresh food and vegetables. It was a great joy to eat food which had not been cooked over an open charcoal fire. Tea and coffee are grown on the slopes of Wellington and Ootacamundoo. There is a notable railway to the Hill Station. It is one of the 'great little railways' shown on the television from time to time. The trees and scrubs around are beautiful. Night jasmine filled the warm night air with a delightful perfume. I learnt to play golf and squash in Wellington. Facilities were ideal. Army transport assisted if we were going to other medical sections in the area. Otherwise you rode a bicycle or had a ride in a rickshaw, but the latter was only taken if you were in a party, it was unwise to ride alone.

The sick patients in the British Military Hospital in Wellington, South India, were chiefly convalescents sent from Base Hospitals in other parts of India, i.e., Secunderabad, Poona, etc. The soldiers had served in Burma and had been badly wounded both mentally and had limbs, i.e., legs or arms removed or severe skull wounds. They were having rehabilitation treatment, and it was rewarding work to see their progress. There was a large maternity and family wing. This was for officers' and other ranks' wives, whose husbands were serving in India before the outbreak of the war.

On 8th May 1945, the war in Europe was over. We did not celebrate because the war in the East was still in progress, although a rumour was circulating that something was about to take place. Then, on 6th August 1945, we heard about the atomic bomb that was used. Japan surrendered on 14th August 1945; we were all jubilant because we would be going home to England.

Vocabulary

1. **Inoculations:** Vaccination, immunization
2. **Aircraft carriers:** A large ship that carries aircraft which use it as a base to land on and take off from
3. **Corvettes:** A small fast ship used in war to protect other ships from attack
4. **Boxing Day:** The first day after Christmas day that is not a Sunday. Boxing Day is an official holiday in Britain and some other countries.
5. **Disembarked:** To leave a vehicle, especially a ship or an aircraft, at the end of a journey
6. **Sterilized:** To kill the bacteria in or on something
7. **Tropical diseases:** Diseases found in tropics or tropical areas
8. **Camp bed:** A light narrow bed that you can fold up and carry easily
9. **Inquisitive:** Curious
10. **Cozy:** Warm, comfortable and safe

Reading Comprehension

1. Who was going to control Europe in 1939?
2. What was done in the hospitals when there were air raids at night-time?
3. Who were asking for trained nurses? Why?
4. Who established A.N.S.? For what purpose?
5. What was exciting for the speaker but upsetting for her parents?
6. How many types of ships were there in Scotland?
7. Under which adverse conditions did she work in operation theatres?
8. Which country did the patients belong to?
9. What was taught to the nurses during their training?
10. Name the wild animals the nurses had to live with.

Language

Study the following sentences:

1. After about one month, I **was informed** that I had to report to the Examination School in Oxford and live in Lincoln College.
2. I **was given** a full medical examination and various inoculations.
3. After six weeks, a number of us Nursing Sisters **were sent** on embarkation leave (I think it was for two weeks).

4. On our return to Oxford, we obtained our tropical uniform and eventually **were given** orders to be prepared to move on.

All the above mentioned sentences use passive voice. Passive voice uses verb 'to be' with third form of verb. We use passive voice when the action is more important than the doer.

Exercise

Change the voice:

1. Why did you miss this opportunity?
2. Transfer these people to our new office.
3. A doctor should see him.
4. Has the agreement been signed by you?
5. Inform the police of the accident.
6. Someone should reply this letter.
7. The committee has issued the report.
8. We should keep our promises.

Pronunciation Practice: Getting your vowel sounds right.

Please pronounce the words in pairs and practise:

fair/far	first/fast
stare/star	thirst/thrust
care/car	hard/heard
heart/hurt	beard/bard
start/strut	card/curd
cart/curt	shirt/shut
set/sat	sit/seat
bet/bat	bit/beat
bed/bad	bid/bead
dead/dad	did/deed
peck/pack	pick /peak
ate/at	it/eat
led/lad	lid/lead

Writing

Here is a chart. Study the patient's chart carefully and write down a report on the condition of the patient. Imagine that you are writing the report after you are done with your shift.

Parameters	6.00am	12.00	15.00 hrs	21.00hrs
Fever	97.2°F	96.0°F	96.4°F	98.4°F
Blood Pressure	120/90	120/90	110/80	120/90
Urine Discharge	500 ml	500 ml	250 ml	800 ml
Fluid Input	250 ml	250 ml	100 ml	1.2 litres

The patient had no sign of fever. Hypertension was controlled with anti-hypertensive drugs (Amlodepine 5 mg).

3 A Doctor for All Seasons

Kavery Nambisan

A successful doctor has few **inauspicious** events to look back on. Criticism from a patient must rank as the worst of these. Dr Noshir Antia delighted in saying that the greatest gift he ever received was from a leprosy patient who threw a prosthetic shoe at him, saying it did not suit his needs. 'I was pleased to have so well rehabilitated him that he could express himself without fear'. His other awards included the Padma Shri and the Hunterian Professorship, which the Royal College of Surgeons, London bestows on a choiced few from around the world.

N.H. Antia represented everything positive in our profession. Until his death on June 26, in Pune, at 85, he fought for the betterment of the poor and of medical methods. In surgery he strove for efficiency, scientific accuracy, flawless technique and dedication. As a plastic surgeon, he did reconstructive surgery that helped hundreds of leprosy and burns patients.

In the last few years he forged links with Bangladesh. A few weeks before his death, he visited the country for the 35th anniversary of a community health initiative he had worked with. He set up rural health projects in Maharashtra where many young doctors learned how to work and innovate in the villages.

Antia was also chiefly responsible for many of the pro-people healthcare decisions that were made by Indian Governments. Much as he **abhorred** politicians, he saw it as his duty to engage with them to make an equitable health policy a reality. He met Prime Minister Manmohan Singh, and other Ministers and bureaucrats, many times to influence the national agenda on health.

Meeting Dr Antia

I was lucky to have made his acquaintance five years ago. I introduced myself to him during lunch at a conference of rural surgeons. He asked me about myself and my work and then said, 'Why don't you join me?' That was his style: direct and **uncluttered** by formality. I did not join him, knowing I had the energy and boldness to attempt only a few of the things that he would want me to do. Every time we met, I was amazed by his vitality, his **trenchant** wit, his sharp grasp of current trends in medicine (and everything else) and his refusal to consider himself special.

Noshir Antia was born on February 8 1922, to Parsi parents, who lived in a small village near Hubli. He often talked with happiness about this period. 'Not much money, no electricity and the bullock cart the only means of transport,' he said. 'But plenty of everything else'.

After school he went to Fergusson College, Pune, and the Government Medical College, Bombay. He won the Fellowship of the Royal College of Surgeons, London, and worked for nine years learning plastic and reconstructive surgery. He came back to work with Dr Coyajee in Pune, one of the best plastic surgeons in the country. Later he moved to the J.J. Group of Hospitals in Bombay and became the Head of the Tata Unit of Plastic Surgery in 1960.

At thirty-eight, he was young to be in such a senior position but he soon proved his leadership. He once told me how tough it was to change the mindset of doctors regarding leprosy. 'When I started to admit my leprosy patients into general wards, the Hospital warned me that there would be a public outcry,' he said. 'But of course there wasn't. It was only the doctors who were afraid'. He had the courage to take risks, a virtue that is perhaps the hallmark of true leadership.

Importance of Research

Antia recognized the importance of research in medicine and set up the Foundation for Medical Research (FMR) in Bombay in 1974. A man remarkably free of pettiness, he made friends with all. He was greatly influenced by the educationist J.P. Naik and the activist Anna Hazare and often spoke of them with affection and gratitude. Of course, his greatest friend was his wife Arnie, a charming lady deeply interested in his ideas and projects. They were lucky enough to have had 50 years together. After his death, it was obvious that she was not going to waste time in grieving. She talked eagerly about the future prospects of the organisations he had set up and about his soon-to-be published autobiography. It was great good fortune that Dr Antia completed his memoirs a few months before he died.

What Antia managed to do in 27 years after retirement was remarkable. Having seen the need of rural areas and of the disadvantaged everywhere, he established many rural health projects in the Pune area that are models of their type. He was a great believer in the inherent strengths of rural women and his projects ensured that they were taught self-reliance. Under his supervision the Foundation for Research in Community Health (FRCH) served as the research secretariat for the Government's path-breaking Health For All project, which gave vision, shape and direction to primary health care in India. 'There is India and there is Bharat,' he said. 'The India, which shines, has everything. Our work must be for Bharat, which has been ignored'.

He strove to make people aware of the Right to Information Act; he was one of the founding members of the Association of Rural Surgeons of India and served as one of its early Presidents; he trained scores of young doctors, health workers, social activists and researchers to take the common sense approach to health.

A year before his death, he handed over the **stewardship** of FRCH to a doctor who had started to work with him 35 years ago, Dr Nergis Mistry.

Dr Noshir Antia was a rare genius with a refined academic and emotional intelligence. I was saddened by the fact that one who did so much to make community health and preventive medicine a reality should die of malaria, a very preventable disease.

But, knowing him, I think he would have said, 'Now there's a challenge. You do something that will help diagnose and **eradicate** malaria instead of writing about me'.

Vocabulary

1. **Inauspicious:** Discouraging
2. **Abhor:** Hate
3. **Uncluttered:** Without unnecessary items
4. **Trenchant:** Sharp
5. **Stewardship:** An act of taking care of
6. **Eradicate:** Wipe out

Reading Comprehension

1. What criticism did Dr Antia receive from a patient?
2. State Dr Antia's work profile in brief.
3. What were some prestigious awards received by Dr Antia?
4. What was Dr Antia's style of interaction?
5. Enumerate some personality traits of Dr Antia.
6. 'There is India and there is Bharat. The India which shines has everything. Our work must be for Bharat, which has been ignored'. Explain.

Countable and Uncountable Nouns

Countable

Countable nouns are easy to recognize. They are things that we can count. For example: 'pen'. We can count pens. We can have one, two, three or more pens. Here are some more countable nouns:

- dog, cat, animal, man, person
- bottle, box, litre

- coin, note, dollar
- cup, plate, fork
- table, chair, suitcase, bag

Countable nouns can be singular or plural:

- My **dog is** playing.
- My **dogs are** hungry.

We can use the indefinite article **a/an** with countable nouns:

- **A** dog is **an** animal.

When a countable noun is singular, we must use a word like **a/the/my/this** with it:

- I want **an** orange. (*not* I want orange.)
- Where is **my** bottle? (*not* Where is bottle?)

When a countable noun is plural, we can use it alone:

- I like oranges.
- Bottles can break.

Uncountable

Uncountable nouns are substances, concepts, etc. that we cannot divide into separate elements. We cannot 'count' them. For example, we cannot count 'milk'. However, we can count 'bottles of milk' or 'litres of milk'. Here are some more uncountable nouns:

- music, art, love, happiness
- advice, information, news
- furniture, luggage
- rice, sugar, butter, water
- electricity, gas, power
- money, currency

We usually treat uncountable nouns as singular. We use a singular verb. For example:

- **This** news **is** very important.
- Your luggage **looks** heavy.

Exercise

Change the following sentences into plural:

1. A teacher is sometimes strict to students.
2. A lesson is not always easy for learners.
3. A cricketer likes to play cricket.
4. My friend loves singing.
5. Furniture of this house is old.

Pronunciation: Silent Letters

B is silent in a word when it is preceded by 'm' or followed by 't' at the final position, e.g., in 'climb', 'thumb', 'doubt'; *d* is silent in a word when it is followed by 'j' or 'g', e.g., in 'adjust', 'adjoin' and in some other words; *k* is silent in a word when it is followed by 'n' at the initial position, e.g., 'knight' 'knife'; *w* is silent at the final position and it is also silent at the initial position when it is followed by 'r' or sometimes when followed by 'h', e.g., 'wrong', 'write', etc.

Practise speaking the following words with correct pronunciation. Find the letters which are silent in these words:

bomb	crumb	plumb	jamb	comb
tomb	dumb	numb	lamb	womb
debt	adjacent	adjective	badge	judge
pledge	fridge	knowledge	edge	porridge
sludge	bridge	handkerchief	handsome	pneumonia
psychology	psalm	pseudo	psyche	
Ptolemaic	empty	resign	foreign	gnat
sign	assign	ghost	aghast	wallah
oh	ah	know	knee	kneel
knit	knave	knot	knob	knock
castle	hustle	glisten	soften	often
listen	fasten	kitchen	batch	catch
latch	watch	debut	buffet	depot
bouquet	wreath	wrong	flow	snow
wrap	show	wrinkle	draw	

Writing

'An angry patient threw a prosthetic shoe at Dr Antia, saying it did not suit his needs'. Considering yourself as the patient, narrate the experience describing Dr Antia's reaction to this criticism.

4 Aarohi: Himalayan Care

Nestled at seven thousand feet above the sea-level is a small village called Satoli. You wouldn't even know about Satoli and the impressive view that it has to offer. It is on the road to Mukteshwar, famous for the vetenirary research institute, the *jaali*—a rockface with a seven and a half thousand feet drop and the **panoramic** view of the snow peaks. It is in the Nainital district and as you climb towards Mukteswar from Mona, you come across this lovely school on right and a notice board that announces *Aarohi*.

You climb to the office, a brick and wood building, with door-panels carved by local artisans. The carvings, called *likhai*, belong to a dying tradition of the Kumaon hills. There is an out-patient department, a clinical-pathology unit, a dispensary, a radio diagnosis unit and the leadership of Dr Sushil Sharma—the founder of Aarohi. In the ninetees, Sushil and his wife Oona came to the hills and started this non-profit organisation.

The healthcare programme of Aarohi was started as a modest curative service with the **inception** of the organization. The team consisted of two locals and the resident doctor. The boy was trained on the job as a laboratory technician and the girl was trained as a nurse. This small service continued for three years and provided essential out-patient treatment for people living in the neighboring 25 odd villages. Emergency service was available round the clock and proved vital at a time when no such facility existed in the area.

The harsh mountain **terrain**, poor accessibility to the nearest District Hospital in Almora along with ignorance and poverty made **morbidity** and mortality levels high. Maternal and infant deaths were common. The tradition of Traditional Birth Attendants (TBAs) was dying and as the bearers of traditional knowledge were getting old, the newer generation was losing this vital source of knowledge.

It was then decided that this knowledge be revived and revitalized and be given a sound scientific **underpinning**. These issues were discussed in open village meetings but found little favour amongst the people since their felt needs focused more on obvious issues like availability of drinking water, sanitation, fodder and fuel wood and livelihoods. The spread of the work was in an organic manner and extended to 12 villages, where the prime criterion used was interest expressed by concerned women. To date, the programme has involved the training of 24 TBAs who are now independently handling deliveries in and around their villages.

Training for these TBAs initially focused on safe deliveries and **perinatal** care and then included other important health issues like family planning, dental care, menstrual hygiene, general hygiene, personal and environmental sanitation, the management of diarrhoea and pneumonia and first aid for common problems. The TBAs have also recognized the limits of their knowledge and capabilities and know when to refer a patient.

After two years of this training, an impact study was done in the initial five villages. The **percolation** of the knowledge of the TBAs in their own community was found to be less than what had been expected. The strategy was reviewed and a concentrated effort was made to spread health awareness through various women's groups like the Self Help Groups, pre-primary schools and youth groups. The health team developed its own communication skills in the field by using puppets to deliver health messages. While the women's groups have involved close to 100 women from seven odd villages over the last three years, the school health programme has consistently dealt with some 1000 children from 20 schools of the area.

The health centre of Aarohi is currently providing out-patient services to about 2000 patients every year from 40 neighboring villages and round the clock emergency services.

About 80 per cent of the medical surgical and gynecological problems are being handled by the centre and the remaining 20 per cent are evacuated to the neighboring district hospitals. The centre has a diagnostic laboratory that can perform basic stool, urine, blood and sputum examinations. It has its own pharmacy that stocks essential drugs for a requirement of six months. A 20 mA portable X-Ray unit takes care of Emergency radio diagnostic needs.

Funds for running the project have been raised from various national and international donor agencies and is currently being funded by the Sir Ratan Tata Trust in Mumbai.

Aarohi also runs a nature shop near the school. Apart from selling herbs, apricot scrubs, and naturally extracted oil they also sell bhujapatra (the ancient papyrus in India) paintings. Arohi ties up with other non-profits and sells their products as well. You get some great pickles and beautiful shawls. On a cold day they might to treat you with thyme tea and jaggery cookies.

Oona is no longer there. She passed away recently. Pradeep Gupta, a banker from Uttar Pradesh along with his wife, Shubha look after the affairs. They are a great support to Sushil who still spends time with Arohi. Pradeep and Subha have built their home in Satoli. It is a quaint old bungalow with a small garden and a big walnut tree. Standing on the verandah of the bungalow, one can view the snow clad mountain peaks. It is a hundred and eighty degree view and something that one can't easily forget. Aarohi is a fitting tribute to the spirit of peace that these mountains instill in you.

Vocabulary

1. **Nestled:** Settled comfortably. Here, the word applies to the village of Satoli. It imagines the village to be alive like a human being.
2. **Panoramic:** A view that spreads over a wide frame
3. **Inception:** Beginning; from the starting point
4. **Terrain:** The geographical nature of a territory
5. **Morbidity:** State of being unwell
6. **Underpinning:** Basis, foundation
7. **Perinatal:** The period around the time of the birth of a child
8. **Percolation:** In sciences, it concerns the movement and filtering of fluids through porous materials. In the text, it stands for the passing on of knowledge to people or futher generation.

Reading Comprehension

1. Who are the founders of Aarohi?
2. What was the nature of medical services offered by Aarohi at the time of its inception?
3. What are the dying traditions that the above passage discusses?
4. What contributed to the high mortality rate in the villages that Aarohi served?
5. How did Aarohi seek to negotiate the issues of perinatal mortality? Why do you think they chose the kind of strategy that they employed?
6. How important is communication in the kind of work that Aarohi undertook?
7. What are the kinds of medical facilities that the Aarohi healthcare unit can now use?
8. How has the nature shop become a part of the goals that Aarohi has?

Language

Read the following sentences:

1. The team **consisted of** two local and a resident doctor.
2. The boy was **trained on the job** as a laboratory technician and the girl was trained as a nurse.
3. This small service **continued for** three years and provided essential out-patient treatment for the people **living in** the neighboring 25 odd villages.
4. Emergency service was available round the clock and proved vital **at a time** when no such facility existed in the area.

The highlighted portions are ***prepositional phrases****. A prepositional phrase consists of a preposition and an object of the preposition.*

Exercise

Make sentences using the following prepositional phrases:

1. Insisted on
2. Serve at
3. Beg for
4. Search into

Pronunciation: Spelling Sequence

Spelling sequence 'ch' may be pronounced /tʃ/, /k/ or /ʃ/; 'ss' may be pronounced /s/, /z/ or /s/ and 'th' is pronounced /θ/ or /ð/ but in English names it is pronounced as /t/. Spelling sequence 'ng' is pronounced as /ŋ/ at the final position; at the medial position also if the word has been derived from a verb or when the plural maker 's' is added to nouns ending in / ŋ/ but it is pronounced as /ŋg/ if the words are not derived from verbs.

Find out the pronunciation of the following words from a dictionary:

Thames	Thailand	Thomas	Thompson
change	chamber	chord	machine
chef	session	classes	assert
assist	dissolve	dessert	mission
aggression	chorus	sing	wrong
ring	long	longing	hunger
singing	bringing	songs	rings
things	cuttings	longer	finger
anger	hanger		

Writing

Imagine that you made a visit to a rehabilitation centre at Shimla. Narrate the experiences of your visit as a unique exposure of your life.

5 Communication in Healthcare: The Perspective of a Nurse

Pre-operative Advice to Patients Before Surgery

Nurses spend more time with patients than doctors and hence can be very helpful in **counselling** patients the night before surgery. This helps in relieving the patient's **anxiety** and **apprehension** about the surgery. Nurses also play a great role in providing information to the patient's family/relatives before, during and after surgery. Here are a few guidelines which could help them convey the right information to the patient and their family:

- Greet the patient with a smile and inform them that their surgery is scheduled tomorrow.
- Tell them that you have seen many such surgeries and watched how patients recover swiftly. This helps to remove anxiety, and your patient gains confidence in you.
- Ask for an **addiction** history and advise them not to smoke or consume alcohol the night before the surgery.
- Ask the patient whether he/she is taking any medicines and if so for what illness.
- Ask whether he/she has any history of diabetes, hypertension, bronchial asthma, loose denture or any previous episode of anesthetic complication during surgery.
- Tell your patient to have food, water or medicines after the midnight before surgery. The only exception is antihypertensive medication which has to be taken in on the morning of surgery. Talk to the doctor for further clarification.
- Check his vital signs.
- Don't forget to record all the above information in the case history file.

- Check the case file for documents like: Blood Requisition, Anesthetic Checkup Certificate, Cardiologist Report, Laboratory Investigation Reports, and last but not the least, check whether Consent Form has been signed.
- Convey the patient's family about the surgery schedule and try to make them comfortable without being **trivial**. For example, there is no risk involved, complications don't occur and the surgeon is god!
- Note down their contact number so that they can be contacted in case of emergency.

Here is a sample of communication between a patient and a nurse on the evening before the patient is scheduled for abdominal surgery for removal of tumors:

Nurse: Good evening, Mrs Sen, Dr Ranjan is going to operate on you next morning.

Mrs Sen: Good evening, sister, when are they going to take me to the Operation Theatre?

Nurse: You've been placed on call from nine in the morning. They'll call you any time after nine. But, we expect it to be around ten o'clock. So, you should not eat anything after dinner. We'll administer a **laxative** and you might need to use the washroom frequently after that. However, there's nothing to worry. If you feel weak and dizzy, do call for an attendant. Do not try to go to the washroom on your own. After your dinner is over, do not take any water, dessert, snack or even medicines. We'll put you on intravenous fluids (dextrose saline) so that you don't dehydrate. By the way, what are the medicines that you're taking?

Mrs Sen: Sister, I'm on Amlodipine, and I need to take it next morning. I also take a sedative after dinner as I have chronic neuropathy.

Nurse: Please do take Amlodipine. It is advised for hypertension. And, you've been specifically advised against any sedative.

Mrs Sen: Is the surgery going to be painful? Are they going to chloroform me?

Nurse: Well, we do not use chloroform. The anesthetist will probably sedate you by injecting a drug into your spine. It is going to be painless. In fact, the anesthetist will ensure that you recover from **sedation** once the surgery is over. You may need to be in a High Dependency Unit managed by the Anesthesia department once the surgery is over.

Mrs Sen: This is my first surgery and I am a bit nervous.

Nurse: Mrs Sen, I have seen at least a hundred people go through an abdominal surgery for removing tumors. These are very simple procedures, and since you do not have diabetes and are not a known cardiac, you'll do well. Your lung function is good and after your surgery, you will need to exercise with an incentive spirometer. You will also need to inhale steam. This will expand your lung cells and prevent them from acquiring pneumonia. Since the surgical wound makes breathing difficult, we tend to shorten our breath allowing our lung to become infected. The more you exert your lung, the more you breathe out bad air.

Mrs Sen: The doctor had asked my family to keep two units of blood ready. We've arranged for donor cards.

Nurse: Thanks a ton! The ward attendant will come and collect those cards from you. Have you signed the consent form?

Mrs Sen: Yes, I have. Here you go. But, tell me something: why do you need this?

Nurse: Well, Mrs Sen, every surgery has an element of risk and we need to record the fact that you are aware of this risk. Moreover, we also need to record the fact that you understand the kind of surgery our doctors are going to perform on you. To operate on a patient without informing them about the nature and risk of the surgery is unethical.

Mrs Sen: Am I going to survive the surgery. Do be honest with me, sister.

Nurse: While we do not deny risks, let me assure you that our healthcare facility is fully equipped to manage all kinds of postoperative crises. We have ventilators, dialysis units and intensive cardiac care units. Finally, the benefits outweigh the risks. There is no chance that you are going to live with this tumor. There is every possibility that once your tumor is relieved, you are going to go places without your needing to take painkillers and anti-hypertension pills!

Mrs Sen: Thanks, Sister for taking time to explain all this to me.

Nurse: It was my pleasure and you are most welcome to ask us all sorts of questions. Now that dinner has arrived you must have that soon. After you've had your dinner, do call us for administering the laxative. Thanks for cooperating. May I take your leave?

Mrs Sen: Yes, and thanks once again

Nurse: It was my pleasure.

Vocabulary

1. **Counselling:** Professional advice
2. **Anxiety:** Nervousness
3. **Apprehension:** Fear
4. **Addiction:** A strong habit
5. **Trivial:** Unimportant
6. **Laxative:** Drug to activate bowel movements
7. **Sedation:** Act of giving a sedative, i.e., a tranquilizer

Reading Comprehension

1. How important is pre-operative counseling for patients by nurses?
2. What details of a patient's history should nurses take from their patients?
3. What documents of a patient should be checked before a surgery?
4. Does Mrs Sen seem to be nervous before her surgery?
5. How does the nurse relieve Mrs Sen of her pre-operative anxiety?

Language: Interrogative Sentence

An interrogative sentence is a type of sentence which usually asks a question and uses a question mark (?). They may ask for information or for confirmation or denial of a statement. They typically begin with a question word such as **what, who, or how,** or an **auxiliary verb such as do/does, can or would,** etc. In English an interrogative sentence normally changes the word order so that the verb or part of the verb comes before the subject.

For example:

- What are the medicines that you are taking?
- Is the surgery going to be painful?
- Have you signed the Consent Form?

Exercise

Change the following sentences into Interrogative:

1. Ask the patient whether he/she is taking any medicines and if so for what illness.
2. Ask whether he/she has any history of diabetes, hypertension and bronchial asthma.
3. Ask whether he/she has deposited the surgery advance.
4. Ask whether a relative or a friend will be present in the waiting room during surgery.

Pronunciation: Letters 'r,' 'g,' 't' and 's':

R is silent when it is preceded by a vowel or at the final position but *r* is pronounced when it follows a vowel. Letter 'g' may be pronounced /g/, /dʒ/; 't' may be pronounced as /t/ or /ʃ/ and 's' is pronounced as /s/, /z/ or /ʒ/:

park	occur	church	charm
drive	crave	marine	curry
car	sir	near	mete
gain	green	generous	gym

mirage	rouge	late	stale
nature	capture	mention	edition
scene	system	busy	these
vision	pleasure		

Writing

Write a conversation between a patient's relative and a nurse discussing the post surgery care to be taken after a successful abdominal surgery.

6 Private and Public Partnership in Healthcare

Bharathi Ghanashyam

Public-private partnerships have sprung up in several states in India to deliver primary healthcare to rural populations. Bharathi Ghanashyam takes a look at one example and asks experts whether similar partnerships should be scaled up to cover the country's entire health sector.

Pattanayakanahalli village lies at a distance of about 172 km from Bangalore on the Bangalore–Mumbai highway in Southern India, 18 km from the nearest town. It is home to a population that is largely made up of landless farmers and small farm holders. Most of these people live below the **poverty line** and earn less than US$420 each year. The village houses a government Primary Health Centre (PHC) that provides services to 47 surrounding villages, and a population of around thirty nine thousand people 24 hours a day, seven days a week.

It is 12 noon and the outpatient department in the PHC is overflowing with people who have come in with common **ailments**.

33-year-old Satyamma, however, is not just a routine patient. She has been married for 16 years and is childless. After two abortions and the death of one child who was born with abnormalities, she is in the third month of her fourth pregnancy and is anxious how it will progress. The gynaecologist who is visiting from Bangalore examines her and reassures her that all will be well. Satyamma is under the care of a private gynaecologist and has come in only for a second opinion. At the end of the examination, she shyly inquires whether she can continue visiting the PHC for the rest of her pregnancy.

Another patient—66-year-old Kadirappa—is recovering from tuberculosis and is on the Directly Observed Treatment (DOTS) regimen. He recalls his innumerable trips in the past to private doctors, who he says, merely offered him **symptomatic treatment**. At the end of two months he had spent around ₹2 000 ($46), which he had to borrow, and was much worse off than he was when he began treatment. A relative referred him to the PHC where his condition was diagnosed.

Two months later, he is feeling much better and, with encouragement from the PHC staff, he says he will complete his treatment.

Nagaraj, who has recovered from tuberculosis, has just been diagnosed as HIV positive. He was tested for HIV/AIDS as part of the routine screening for tuberculosis patients at the PHC. The test was done after he was counselled at the integrated counselling and testing centre at the PHC. He is now being persuaded to begin **antiretroviral** treatment as his CD4 cell count has fallen below desirable levels.

Satyamma, Kadirappa and Nagaraj have one thing in common—they have all used the facilities offered by the Pattanayakanahalli PHC, some of which are unique to it and are not offered at other PHCs. This is because the PHC is being run in a public-private partnership between two entities: Karuna Trust—a public charitable trust based in Bangalore—and the Government of Karnataka—a southern state of India.

Karuna Trust also manages 25 other PHCs across the state of Karnataka, as well as nine in Arunachal Pradesh in northeast India. It has ensured that PHCs under its management provide round-the-clock emergency and casualty services, outpatient facilities six days a week, a five to ten bed in-patient department, and 24-hour labour and essential obstetric facilities. Additionally, the Trust has introduced **innovations** such as integration of mental health services, eye care, and specialist services at the primary care level.

Karuna Trust has come a long way since taking over the management of its first PHC at Gumballi in Karnataka in 1996 (see table). Its success has led the Karnataka Government to issue a formal policy on public–private partnerships in 2000.

India is a signatory to the Alma-Ata Declaration, which calls for 'Health for All' to be achieved in countries through a primary healthcare approach. In 1983, the country's National Health Policy adopted the Alma-Ata definition of primary healthcare to mean the provision of curative, preventive, promotive, and rehabilitative health services. This development was a shift from curative to integrated healthcare with an emphasis on increasing access to health services in rural areas.

To give form to this commitment, a huge infrastructure was established, consisting of a three tier system, that is, primary, secondary, and tertiary care. PHCs are units that provide integrated rural healthcare and also provide **referral** to secondary and tertiary care. Each PHC covers a population of 20 to 30 thousand. India has about 23 000 PHCs, 1 30000 subcentres, and one lakh fifty thousand healthcare institutions. Karnataka alone has two thousand one hundred ninty three PHCs. The state of these centres, however, leaves much to be desired.

Hanumappa Sudarshan, founder of Karuna Trust says, 'Notwithstanding the infrastructure available, all is not well with the primary healthcare system. It has become **decrepit** and use of PHCs has fallen to **abysmal** levels, thereby necessitating the involvement of civil-society organisations to shore up the deficiencies'.

Studies indicate that only 69 per cent of PHCs in India have at least one bed. Absence rates among health workers range between 35–58 per cent in different

Indian states. Devi Shetty, chairman of the Narayana Hurudayalaya Institute of Cardiac Studies, points out:

> Insufficient staff, unavailability of essential drugs, and other problems at government-run PHCs make it difficult for rural communities to get treatment and they are forced to purchase healthcare services from private practitioners. The greater danger, however, is that they will delay accessing treatment for fear of losing wages and bearing out-of-pocket expenses.

He speaks from ground-level experience, since his institution has established, and runs PHCs as part of a pilot programme in Amethi in Uttar Pradesh.

The National Family Health Survey 2005–06 revealed that 46 per cent of children below the age of three years are underweight. India's infant mortality rate is 57 per 1000 livebirths and its maternal mortality ratio is 301 per 100000 livebirths and should be reduced to below 42 and 109, respectively, to achieve Millennium Development Goals 4 and 5 on child and maternal health. India also has the largest pool of never-immunized children in the world—9·4 million. These are results that the primary healthcare system must account for. Despite its firm commitment to providing primary healthcare, why has India failed on so many counts? Madabhushi Madan Gopal, secretary of the Health and Family Welfare Department, Karnataka says, 'The government lacks managerial skills and professionalism. We have also fallen behind in establishing community **rapport** and enabling **convergence** between the various departments that look at health, water, and sanitation, etc'.

Since public-private partnerships translate into benefits for those seeking healthcare, should they be scaled-up to cover the entire sector? Sudarshan disagrees firmly:

> Primary healthcare is the responsibility of the state. PPPs [public–private partnerships] are not alternatives to poor governance and leadership. Even with the PHCs we manage, there are variable degrees of progress. In districts where the District Health Officer understands the rationale of the PPP and provides constructive leadership, the progress has been tremendous. In others, progress has been slow. PPPs can work only with the support of strong, honest, and able governance.

Devi Shetty, however, strikes a different note:

> I believe that primary healthcare must be offered free, but it is not mandatory for the government to do this. Governments across the world have failed in providing free primary healthcare to the community. Private players can provide better services as they operate to economies of scale and bring in professionalism. If health insurance becomes mandatory, primary health services offered by the private sector will translate into benefits for the poor.

Madan Gopal believes,

> primary healthcare must never be sold and, as a nation, we cannot afford profit at the expense of the poor. We need long-term planning and sustainable policies,

as well as greater spending on healthcare. Partnerships to share skills and not substitution by business enterprises are what we require additionally. Most importantly, we need a community-centred approach to the health sector, as spelt out in the Alma-Ata Declaration, so that the community has a greater say and can force change.

Whether the primary healthcare in India will be opened up to the private sector remains to be seen. It is, however, a healthy sign that debate has begun.

Vocabulary

1. **Poverty line**: The official level of income that is necessary to buy the basic necessities of life such as food, clothes, etc.
2. **Ailments:** Illnesses that are not very serious
3. **Symptomatic treatment**: A cure that depends on the external signs of a disease instead of its causes
4. **Innovations**: New ways of doing thing
5. **Antiretroviral**: A retrovirus is a virus that gets into the cell and reverses the general function of the cell which is to transcript DNA into RNA and RNA getting translated into proteins
6. **Referral:** A healthcare facility where patients are sent by doctors for better treatment
7. **Decrepit**: Old, feeble, not in good condition or health
8. **Abysmal:** Extremely bad or of a very low standard
9. **Rapport:** A friendly relationship between communities or people that helps in professional work
10. **Convergence**: Meeting point of different directions or angles. In this case, it means the meeting of different public offices on the common goal of providing primary healthcare.

Reading Comprehension

1. Define poverty line in keeping with the bench-mark the author of the above passage has employed.
2. Quote one sentence from the second paragraph of the passage that suggests that the PHC at Pattanayakahalli is different from other such agencies. (*Hint: It has something to do with the patient called Satyamma*)
3. Discuss three kinds of roles of the Karuna trust.
4. Discuss the state of affairs of the PHCs in India. Bring in data into your discussuion. You also need to talk about the problems that plague the PHCs.
5. Is private-public partnership the only way to make primary healthcare functional in India? Can you think of any problem that privatization entails?

Language

An *article* belongs to a word-class called *determiners*. They precede a noun and tell us whether the referent is *definite* or *indefinite*. In other words if a noun is the name of something, the article lets us know whether the thing can be identified specifically or not.

Now read the following passage:

India is a[1] signatory to the[2] Alma-Ata Declaration, which calls for 'Health for All' to be achieved in countries through a[3] primary healthcare approach. In 1983, the[4] country's National Health Policy adopted the Alma-Ata definition of primary healthcare to mean the provision of curative, preventive, promotive, and rehabilitative health services. This development was a shift from curative to integrated healthcare with an[5] emphasis on increasing access to health services in rural areas.

In the above passage, 1, 3 and 5 signal nouns that are either one of many. There are many *signatories* to the Alma-Ata declaration and India is just one of the many. Similarly, there are many *approaches* to ensure that everybody receives healthcare; focusing on primary healthcare is just one of the many approaches. The *emphasis* on increasing access to health services in rural areas is one of the many possible areas of emphasis. On the other hand, 2 and 4 signal specific objects about which there is a consensus between the author and the reader. There can be only one Alma-Ata agreement—it is historically specific event. And, in 1983 there can be only one National Health Policy.

A/an are, thus, indefinite articles that are used with singular and countable nouns. There is also something called a *Φ article*, also known as a *zero article*. It refers to indefinite plurals. Now, re-read the sentence: *This development was a shift from curative to integrated healthcare with an[5] emphasis on increasing access to [Φ] health services in rural areas.* 'Health services' refer to no particular strategy or service (primary healthcare or setting up super-speciality hospitals) and hence we can 'sense' the *zero article*. Understanding the concept of the *zero article* helps us avoid confused use of the definite/indefinite articles.

Exercise

A. Fill in the blanks with the correct article following the instructions in parenthesis:

1. There is __________ stapler on the desk. (no particular stapler)
2. There is ____________ gentleman outside the office of Mrs Dutta. (no particular gentleman)
3. _____ committee on public affairs (a particular committee) was set up by ____ new government. (a specific government)
4. __________ good film (any good film) has to have ________ good script.
5. __________ film that gave me great pleasure was *Shoot the Piano Player*.

B. Fill in the blanks with the correct article:

1. __________ fresh air is needed by all growing children.
2. __________ gust of fresh air can rid us of depression.
3. __________ photocopying machine in our office is seldom in order.
4. We need __________ photocopying machine in our office.
5. _________ moon has been enveloped by clouds. It was _________ gloomy day.
6. _________ cup of hot chocolate is _______ drink you need on a cold and damp day.
7. He likes to study _______ astrophysics.
8. He went to _______ USA to get _________ degree in _________ astrophysics.
9. _________ teaspoon of honey helps _______ lot in _______ winter.
10. This year, we expect ______ good harvest. _____ rains were adequate.

Conveying information and eliciting information: agreeing and disagreeing

The following conversation between a nurse and a doctor is an example of how information ought to be exchanged between them. The conversation also teaches you to agree, disagree and make crucial interventions within a conversation. The doctor often depends on the nurse to understand the criticality of the patient. It is important that the nurse is clear about what she wants to convey.

Nurse: Good Morning Dr Varghese, your patient Mr Nayar is complaining of malaise and fever.

Doctor: Thanks for your prompt attention. Did you check his body temperature?

Nurse: It is 102 degree Fahrenheit. But, yesterday at 10 pm, it was within normal limits.

Doctor: Does he have fever with chill and rigor?

Nurse: The patient is complaining of chill but not rigor.

Doctor: What are the medicines that he is taking, right now?

Nurse: He is on Amlodipine 5 mg daily and Tablet MV once daily. His blood pressure is normal now. But, he has been catheterized for the last nine days.

Doctor: Good that you informed me of this. Prolonged catheterization might lead to urinary tract infection. Send her urine-sample for routine examination and culture sensitivity, please. Do inform the Department of Laboratory Medicine that it is urgent.

Nurse: Sure. Do we need to add any new medicine?

Doctor: Administer tablet Paracetamol 500 mg four times every day and continue with the other drugs. Do call me up when you get the provisional report as the final culture sensitivity test will take time. I will add antibiotics if required.

Nurse: Thank you. I will do as much .Have a good day.

Doctor: Thank you and you have a good day too!

The above conversation teaches you to greet and begin or end a conversation. Observe how the doctor acknowledges information that the nurse passes on to him. Question forms using the 'does…have' form is used to request information. The basic form is to use the do verb with the have verb. In case of a singular subject, we use do + have form. Expressions like will do as much convey a sense of agreement.

Re-read what the doctor has to say in the extract, from the above conversation, that follows

acknowledging information

Good that you informed me of this. Prolonged catheterization might lead to urinary tract infection. Send her urine-sample for routine examination and culture sensitivity, please. Do inform the Department of Laboratory Medicine that it is urgent.

giving instructions in a polite way

In the above conversation, expressions note the use of the do + basic verb form to make requests. Again, adding a please after a comma, as in the second sentence, is a polite but firm way of placing a request.

A communication model that one can follow is this:

Acknowledge information

↓

Instruct politely

↓

Close conversation by greeting and thanking

Practise in pairs

Use the words in the box to form a conversation similar to the one above:

> Stethoscope, gasping patient, ventilator, intensive care unit, shift, Post-operative trauma, cardiovascular surgery, lipid profile check, chest x-ray, creatine phosphokinase test.

Pronunciation: Double consonants

All double consonants except 'cc' are pronounced as single consonant sounds. 'cc' may be pronounced as /ks/ when followed by 'e', 'i', or 'y' or /k/ when followed by the rest of the letters. Check these words in a good dictionary:

rubber	dimmer	letter	running
happy	shabby	committee	funny
swimming	butter	chatter	clutter
accord	accurate	account	accent
access	accident	success	vaccine
accredited	hiccup	acclaim	succumb

Writing

Write a diary-entry about a nurse's day in a ward.

7

Managing Pain

My colleague, Jeff, was not allowed to work on the ward while his mother was an in-patient. The first morning, I cared for Jeff's mother. While walking around the ward to assess the patients under my care, I spoke with her and asked her if she had any pain. She responded, 'No, I am fine', to which I replied, 'Well if you have any pain, please let me know and I can give you some painkillers, if you think you need them'. I then left her and spent time with the other patients, but when I left her bed area to answer the phone, I saw her holding her abdomen and **grimacing**.

I made my way to her bed and asked her how she was feeling. She again replied 'Fine', although her **body language** showed otherwise. I, therefore, commented that I thought she looked uncomfortable and asked her if she was now experiencing any pain. However, she again replied, 'No, I'm fine', but because of her behaviour, I was not convinced and felt that she probably was experiencing some discomfort. I then looked at her drug chart and discovered that she had not had any **analgesia** for over six hours, but obviously, I did not want to keep asking her the same question over and over again.

I, therefore, took a different approach and sat on her bed and started to talk about how she felt in general. We quickly struck up a conversation about how she was feeling and soon established a **rapport**. At this point, I gently asked her if she was uncomfortable to which she finally admitted that she was 'quite uncomfortable'. When I asked her why she had not told me sooner, she replied that she did not want to bother me. I immediately arranged some analgesia for her and emphasized the importance of her telling me if she was experiencing any discomfort in the future.

I didn't think any more of the incident until Jeff arrived on the ward later in the day with his wife and father to visit his mother. We spoke together and I explained how his mother was doing, and I briefly mentioned the incident to him. I felt that, as with many patients, especially the elderly, it was probably due to the fact that she just didn't want to 'trouble me'. However, Jeff explained to me that this roundabout form of communication (particularly the apparent switching from no to yes [or vice versa] and back again) is found in many cultures, especially those in South-east Asia, but is almost never seen in northern Europe, the USA or the UK.

On reflection, I suppose that this particular incident is perhaps an important issue in cross-cultural nursing. However, I was unaware of this kind of behaviour and probably would have never found out about it, unless I'd experienced it first hand. What it did make me realize, though, was the importance of using a range of communication skills, especially when caring for those from a different culture. It really makes me think about how, as nurses, we should communicate with patients in order to acquire important information from them. I'm now aware that good communication is not just about talking, or even listening: it's also about observing and assessing the situation, so that you use the most appropriate approach and skills (verbal and non-verbal) in that situation.

Vocabulary

1. **Grimacing:** An ugly expression made by twisting your face, used to show pain, disgust, etc.
2. **Rapport:** Connection
3. **Analgesia:** Painkiller
4. **Body language:** The process of communicating what you are feeling or thinking by the way you place and move your body rather than by words

Reading Comprehension

1. Who was Jeff? Why was he not allowed to work on the ward?
2. 'No, I am fine.' Why did Jeff's mother say these words?
3. What made the speaker feel that the lady was experiencing some discomfort? How did she find that she was quite uncomfortable?
4. What is good communication? What range of communication skills are the nurses expected to know?

Language

The above narration uses a number of connectives or linking words like *the first morning, while, if, then, and, when, although, therefore, at this point, however,* etc. Connectives are used to indicate order (*first, above all,* etc.); add something (*and, more,* etc.); compare things and ideas (*as, likewise, similarly,* etc.); express reason and purpose (*as, because, hence,* etc.); condition (*if, unless,* etc.); concession (*though, although,* etc.); opposing or limiting statements (*but, however, or*) and contrast (*but, however, nevertheless*) as well to impart continuity to a narrative.

Pronunciation: Sounds /θ/and/ð/

Exercise

Fill in the blanks using the correct connective from the list given below:

1. Karishma is rich, ___ her friend Kirti is poor.
   a. therefore
   b. but
   c. otherwise
2. You'd better take a taxi. ___, you'll be late.
   a. consequently
   b. furthermore
   c. otherwise
3. I enjoy reading this newspaper ___ it has good articles.
   a. because
   b. nevertheless
   c. however
4. Joy was very tired. ___, he took a nap.
   a. otherwise
   b. therefore
   c. nevertheless
5. Pooja wasn't thirsty; ___, she drank three glasses of water.
   a. however
   b. moreover
   c. furthermore
6. The weather was terrible. ___, we decided to delay our trip.
   a. furthermore
   b. besides
   c. therefore
7. You must buy the tickets; ___, we won't be able to see that play.
   a. otherwise
   b. although
   c. besides
8. The neighborhood isn't very interesting. I like the house, ___.
   a. moreover
   b. thus
   c. though
9. We live in the same building; ___, we hardly see each other.
   a. however
   b. therefore
   c. furthermore

Some words have /θ/ sound but their derivatives have /ð/.

10. He didn't earn enough money. ___, his wife decided to get a job.
    a. moreover
    b. therefore
    c. although
11. That house isn't big enough for us, and ___, it's too expensive.
    a. furthermore
    b. hence
    c. although
12. She's not snobbish ___ nobody would like her.
    a. hence
    b. however
    c. otherwise
13. We won't start remodelling the house, ________ we have plenty of money and workers.
    a. nevertheless
    b. unless
    c. thus
14. It was a windy and rainy night. ___, I decided to go out.
    a. nevertheless
    b. otherwise
    c. hence

Say the following pairs of words aloud:

mouth/mouths	youth /youths
bath/ bathe	breath/ breathe
cloth/clothes	wreath/wreathes
north/northern	south/southern
breath/breathe	mouth (n)/mouth (v)
heath / heathen	

Writing

What, according to you, is the importance of communication skills in the nursing profession?

8

Stress in Nursing

Pratibha P. Kane

Stress is experienced when demands made on us outweigh our resources. A moderate level of stress or 'Eustress' is an important motivating factor and is considered normal and necessary. If stress is intense, continuous and repeated, it becomes a negative phenomenon or 'Distress', which can lead to physical illness and psychological disorders. Psychosomatic illnesses are disorders that involve both the body and the mind. These illnesses are mental or emotional in origin and have physical symptoms. Running hospitals as businesses have changed the working pattern of nursing as a whole. Stress levels are on the rise and little is being done about assessing this malady and actively managing its effects. Nurses are expected to give sensitive quality patient care, have patience, and help disposition and, at the same time, save costs and increase efficiency by keeping a rapid throughput.

Nurses are the backbone of any healthcare unit. The pressures of overtime and long working hours create a work–personal life imbalance, which begins to affect the health of employees. Other factors such as long commuting hours and chaotic traffic conditions adding to their stress affect employees' efficiency and effectiveness. It can **undermine** an employee's relationship at home as well as on the job. This can have a negative influence on their physical and emotional health and lead to psychosomatic disorders. Economic loss to the organization due to errors, wrong decisions, wrong choice, lack of attention and injury are some of the serious effects of **chronic** stress. The trend of nurses working overtime started with **downsizing** of organizations and the trend to have only **skeletal manning**. Absenteeism is compensated by others doing overtime. This increases the take-home pay but is likely to injure their health. Such nurses experience severe stress and require more sick leaves. This risk increases with the length of overtime.

All nurses have to do shift work or attend emergencies at night. The stress of shift work can also aggravate health conditions and lead to heart disease or digestive disorders. Fatigue can lead to error, injury and carelessness. Long hours are a source of depression, low morale and low motivation. Shift workers are on the job in the evening or on weekends, and they sleep during the day. Hence, they often miss out on social or family activities.

There is a stark difference in causes of stress in nurses in developed countries and in India. Nurses in India are poorly remunerated compared to the world standards. For the kind of intense work that the nurses do, the salary and benefits are not adequate. The fact that rewards are not proportional to workload is a source of great stress as it is difficult to have decent standards of living based only on their basic salary.

Lack of professional respect and recognition by authorities and doctors is the major cause of dissatisfaction in nurses abroad. Poor relationship with physicians was related to **musculoskeletal disorders**, which is seen as the most important reason for nurses leaving hospitals. Lack of **autonomy**, poor participation in patient care due to lack of sufficient knowledge and **empowerment** deprive them from job satisfaction.

Nurses in India are mainly from the lower economic strata and have low educational qualifications. Their main motivators are salary and benefits to support their home and maintain a decent standard of living. Shortage of staff makes them easily succumb to increasing their pay package by doing excessive hours of overtime at the expense of their health. They have limited access to claims and compensation for occupational hazards.

Many studies of stress in nurse in developed countries have shown chronic stress as a major contributor to suicide or suicidal thoughts, smoking, excessive coffee consumption and alcohol intake.

Resurfacing of repetitive problems and feeling of the work never getting done added to stress in this study. **Turnover** for skilled nurses is **instigated** by internal, on the job factors, which cause dissatisfaction and stress (poor salary, lack of recognition, workplace bullying) and a desire to leave. Replacement is mostly with less-skilled staff, which increases the responsibility and load of the remaining skilled staff. Shortage of staff increases the burden of non-nursing jobs, like shifting patients, picking up food trays, making beds, and even filing and keeping record.

Poor nutrition leading to anaemia contributes to the poor health of the nurses in this study. Meals are usually not taken in time. Missing breaks to finish work also increases stress. Shift work can interfere with regular eating and digestive **circadian rhythm**. This could lead to acidity and other stomach problems. However, digestive problems also could be caused by the tendency for excessive consumption of tea or coffee in the night shift.

In the absence of doctors, nurses are on the front line and have to face verbal abuse from patients and relatives for issues that may not be directly connected to their work. Physical violence and aggressiveness is also on the rise in patients and their relations. Demanding patients and their relatives can cause conflict and lead to more stress. Patients' expectations from nurses are sometimes unreasonable and they tend to be aggressive. No training is given to them to deal with confrontation.

Stress-related illness is not imaginary. It is very tricky to diagnose and treat. The key is to look for a source of stress that the person is not coping with.

Chronic stress decreases motivation. It can lead to increased absenteeism and increased turnover and **attrition** rates. Thus, it is mandatory for healthcare organizations to address this issue urgently. There is urgent need for proactive stress management, especially preventive strategies, as are encouraged in the industry and IT sector. There is need for coping techniques like team building, counseling, learning assertiveness and communication skills, which should be taught to all nurses, even incorporated in their training curriculum.

Elimination of all stressors is a **utopian** goal. Effective solutions can be found, like increasing skills, enriching work, and increasing the participation of nurses in the organization. Adequate staffing, which reduces job stress and overtime, could lead to improved efficiency along with cost effectiveness.

An ounce of prevention is worth a pound of cure: every organization should assess the magnitude of stress and analyse it to recognize the need for action. This is also called a 'stress audit'. Earlier, stress was viewed as a personal problem to be tackled at an individual level with **palliative** or remedial measures. Now, the approach is to be proactive, with emphasis on prevention and elimination rather than treatment. Improving the quality of work life of nurses may go a long way to decrease attrition.

References

1. Feskanich, D., J.L. Hastrup, J.R. Marshall, G.A. Colditz, M.J. Stampfer, W.C. Willett, et al., 2002, 'Stress and Suicide in Nurses Health Study', *J. Epidemiol Community Health*, 56(2): 95–8.
2. O' Brian-Pallas, L., J. Shamian, D. Thomson, C. Alksnis, M. Koehoorn, M. Kerr, et al., 2004, 'Work-related Disability in Canadian Nurses', *J. Nurs Scholarsh*, 36: 352–7.

Vocabulary

1. **Undermine:** Weaken
2. **Chronic:** Persistent
3. **Downsize:** Economize
4. **Musculoskeletal disorder:** Disorders that affect the body's muscles, joints, tendons, ligaments and nerves
5. **Autonomy:** Independence
6. **Empowerment:** Control over one's own life or situation
7. **Turnover:** Earning
8. **Instigate:** Originate

9. **Circadian rhythm:** Rhythm of digestion: keeping time in the gastrointestinal tract
10. **Attrition:** Employee turnover within a company
11. **Utopian:** Idealistic
12. **Palliative:** Soothing

Reading Comprehension

1. When is stress experienced?
2. What are psychosomatic illnesses?
3. What stress factors affect nurses' efficiency and effectiveness?
4. What can be the reasons for job dissatisfaction among nurses?
5. Give the causes of poor health conditions among nurses.
6. Issues related to nurses should be urgently addressed by healthcare organizations. What are they?
7. What is a stress audit?

Language

1. Present Indefinite

[VERB] + s/es in third person

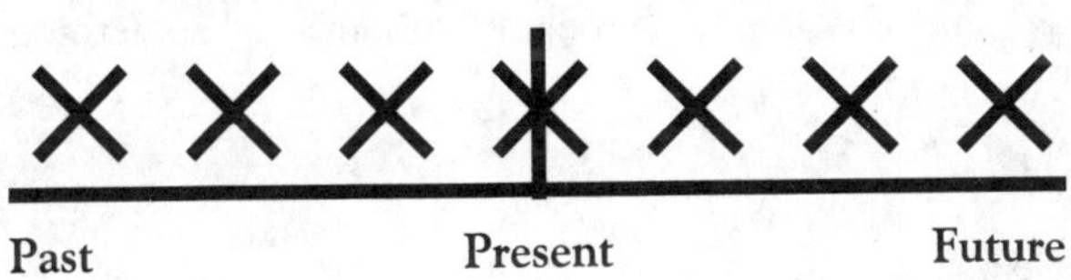

Present Indefinite or Simple Present is used to express the idea that an action is repeated or is usual. The action can be a habit, a hobby, a daily event, a scheduled event or something that often happens or a general truth. It can also be something a person often forgets or usually does not do.

1. To express habitual actions
   - He drinks two cups of coffee every morning.
2. To express general truths
   - Stress is experienced when demands made on us outweigh our resources.
   - Nurses are the backbone of any healthcare unit.
   - The sun rises in the east.
3. In stories, as substitute for Simple Past
   - The thief opens the door and enters the house.

4. To express a future event that is part of a fixed timetable or fixed programme
    - The next train leaves at 6.

Exercise

Use the bracketed verbs in simple present tense:

1. Joanne ____ (work) eight hours a day.
2. Who ____ you ____(speak) to?
3. I ____ (not know) him very well.
4. Your train ____ (leave) at 17.25 from platform 3.
5. Rain seldom ___ (fall) in the Sahara.

2. Present Continuous

(am/is/are + present participle)

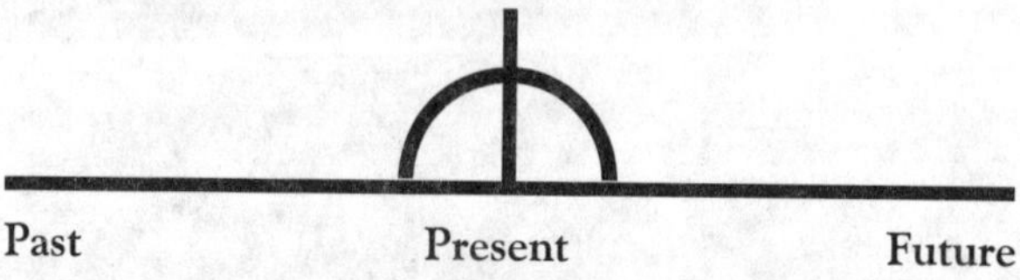

Present Continuous is used with Normal Verbs to express the idea that something is happening now, at this very moment. It can also be used to show that something is not happening now.

Examples:

- You **are learning** English now.
- You **are not swimming** now.
- **Are** you **sleeping**?
- **I am sitting.**
- **Is** he **sitting** or **standing**?
- They **are reading** their books.
- What **are** you **doing**?

Exercise

Use Present Continuous forms of the verbs given in brackets:

1. I (study) to become a doctor.
2. Why you not (do) your homework?
3. She always (come) late to class.
4. He (visit) his parents next weekend.
5. You still (watch) TV.

3. Present Perfect Tense

[has/have + past participle]

Study the following sentences from the text and notice the structure of the items in bold. It is has/have + past participle and this use is of Present Perfect Tense.

- Many studies of stress in nurses **have shown** chronic stress as a major contributor to suicides.
- Running hospitals as business **has changed** the working pattern of nursing as a whole.

We use the Present Perfect to say that an action happened at an unspecified time before now. The exact time is not important. You CANNOT use the Present Perfect with specific time expressions such as: yesterday, one year ago, last week, when I was a child, when I lived in Japan, at that moment, that day, one day, etc. We CAN use the Present Perfect with unspecific expressions such as: ever, never, once, many times, several times, before, so far, already, yet, etc.

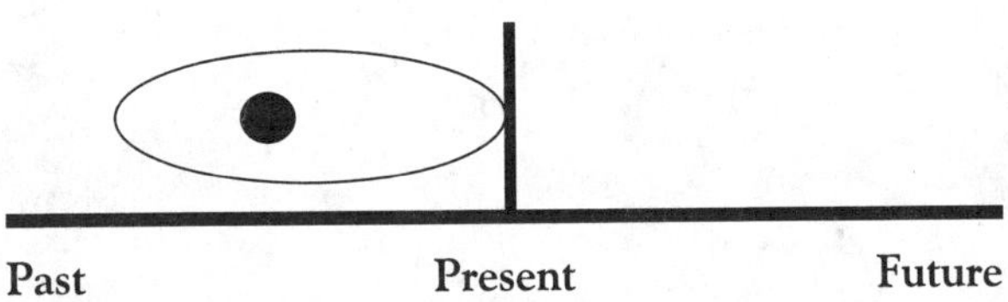

Examples

- I **have seen** that movie twenty times.
- I think I **have met** him once before.
- There **have been** many earthquakes in California.
- People **have travelled** to the moon.
- **Have** you not **read** the book yet?
- Nobody **has** ever **climbed** that mountain.
- I **have had** a cold for two weeks.

Exercise

Fill in the blanks by using the verbs given in brackets in Present Perfect Tense:

1. I **(be)**____ to France.
2. He (never **travel)**____ by train.
3. You ever **(meet)**_____ him?
4. Bill still **(not arrive)**_____.

Past Indefinite and Present Perfect

Sometimes the Past Simple and the Present Perfect are confused. It is important to remember that the Past Simple is used to express a finished past action which occurs at a **specific** moment in the past. The present perfect is used to express something that happened at an **unspecified** moment in the past. For example, if I visited Paris in 2004, I could express this in two ways:

Past Indefinite

I visited Paris in 2004.

- Note that the moment in time is specific—'in 2004', 'a few years ago'.

Present Perfect

I've been to Paris.

In this case, the moment of my visit is not specific. I am speaking about an experience that I have had in my life **up to this moment in time.**

Pronunciation

The following words are commonly mispronounced by non-native speakers of English. Speak them loudly and look for their correct pronunciation in a dictionary:

academic	accept	accommodation	adequatel
advantage	analysis	analytical	apology
apple	assistance	association	atmosphere
balcony	bear	breakfast	bowl
buffalo	calcium	calendar	career
carrier	cassette	celebrity	character
choreography	cigarette	clarity	colleague
compare	compere	competitive	competitor
concept	confusion	crèche	data
develop	dialogue	direction	director
echo	embarrass	enough	enthusiasm
envelop	envelope	environment	ethics
exact	example	except	expect
executive	gigantic	receipt	resume (n)
resume	thorough	tortoise	vehicle
village	wallet	Wednesday	

Writing

Write a letter to the Director, 'World Health Organization', apprising him of the unfavourable working conditions of nurses in developing countries.

9 The Quiet Soldiers of Compassion

If you drive deep into the forested heart of India, 360 kilometres away from Nagpur, you will find nothing but giant mosquitoes and thoughts for company, and occasional **clusters** of huts—mere lashings of damp leaf and grass. It is a beautiful country, an **emerald** world cut by streams and rivers, but it is so lonely, so isolated, you can almost touch its forgottenness. Six hours into this silent receding world and suddenly you come to a white arch—Lok Biradari Prakalp, Hemalkasa. Turn in and the first thing you feel is disappointment. There seems nothing here but the standard issue buildings of middle India—grey cement, green mould. It is dusk and raining hard. A **wiry** man in white vest and white shorts steps up.

'We didn't expect it all to be so large', we say.

'We didn't either', he says and bursts into a hearty laugh. And the miracle of it all starts to reveal itself.

Media and television crews are **thronging** the red-verandah house of Dr Prakash and Manda Amte, both now 60. They have just been declared recipients of the prestigious Magsaysay award—an award that Prakash's revolutionary father, the 'scientific humanist' Baba Amte was himself honoured with over 20 years ago. It is an invitation for the world to come looking for the Amte family legend. Sitting in the gathering darkness, thick moths **swirling** around unreliable lights, the doctors are trying hard to comply, but the legend runs deeper than anecdotes about snake bites and bear attacks, deeper than grainy black and white pictures can tell. The spirit of it is caught for a moment as husband and wife step into the rain under a common umbrella for a community dinner in a common dining hall. The morning brings fresh revelations.

Life at Hemalkasa always begins at dawn with a walk to the Indravati river, two kilometres away—an unfailing ritual, a slice of pleasure, before the urgencies of the day take control. In a sense, it is also a daily return to roots. Thirty-seven years earlier, Baba Amte had brought his wife and sons, Vikas and Prakash, for a rare outing here to Bhamragad, a confluence of three rivers where Baba had roamed as a young boy hunting with the Madia Gonds, the tribe **indigenous** to the region. The picnic would become a crucial turning point. Decades after independence, the Madias were still living in a pitiable condition. As hunter-gatherers, they had little access to regular food, and almost no healthcare—barring the whimsy of witchdoctors. Malaria, tuberculosis, diarroehea, whooping cough, gangrene, ulcers and malnutrition raged among them. The sight of strangers sent them scuttling like startled deer. Baba made an impulsive decision to start work among them.

It took three years for the government to give him 50 acres of land in the heart of the jungle. Baba moved in with a handful of workers and his elder son Vikas in 1973, clearing bits of the hostile land, cutting through stone. About a year later, Prakash cut short his degree in general surgery and joined the project in Hemalkasa. He came with his adopted sister Renuka and his new bride, Mandakini, an anaesthetist and the daughter of RSS pracharaks from Nagpur—not exactly **conventional** material for the **unorthodox** life. They had nothing but two thatched huts to live in, and the fierce jungle around. Baba and the others moved back to other urgent projects scattered across the country. Prakash and Manda and Renuka stayed with a small band of volunteers.

For six months, not a single Madia Gond would come near them. Today, Hemalkasa runs a 50-bed hospital and an OPD that treats over 40 000 Madia tribals a year. It has a residential school up to Class XII for 650 Madia boys and girls and a training programme for barefoot doctors. All of this is free of charge. It also has an animal orphanage—affectionately christened Amte's Ark by a visitor—that houses an astonishing range of wild animals from leopards, lions and bears to crocodiles, wolves, hyenas, snakes, porcupines, badgers, deer and owls—all of them in **lustrous** health, all of them personally looked after by Prakash and some helpers.

None of this reveals itself as immediately extraordinary unless one explores the tenacious will and dedication it took to accomplish it Prakash and Manda Amte tend to a skeletal frame in their open air OPD at Hemalkasa; their grandchild Arunav plays alongside. To live in Hemalkasa in the 1970s meant poverty and **utter isolation**. There was no electricity for 17 years, no supplies, no school, no community. Food meant a simple, unchanging menu of rice and moong dal, darkness meant the hiss of the hurricane lamp. For six months in a year, Hemalkasa was completely cut off when the river Bandia flooded in July. News of the world only came in sporadic gusts when Jagan Mechakale, a **herculean** volunteer, cycled or walked the 60 kilometres from base camp Nagepelli to deliver messages. Once a year, Sadhnatai—Baba's warrior wife—walked the distance herself to see if her youngest and his family were still alive. In 1975, it took several months for Prakash to know that his second son Aniket had been born—and had been sick. When he was barely 18 months old, they almost lost their elder son Diganth to cerebral malaria; he suffered from epileptic fits for years afterwards. Manda, a deceptively strong woman, short on words, high on action, wept then and again years later when all three of her children—Diganth, Aniket and adopted daughter Aarti—consecutively failed their board examinations. Had they done right in choosing this life for their children? 'There was an atmosphere of death in the house when this happened', says Prakash, 'but we absorbed these shocks and kept moving on'.

Ask him what kept him in Hemalkasa through all this, though, and his response is instinctive and quick:

> Manda's companionship—and the people's faith. That is what keeps us here. I have never seen such tolerance for pain. They come to us from a radius of 200 kilometres, we try to help them. Sometimes when I cut their wounds, the pus sprays onto my face and body. We never had gloves but it never mattered. When I watch their wounds—black, poisonous, foul-smelling—slowly turning red and healthy, that is my reward.

This unassuming **compassion**—this life-affirming **gratification** in serving others—is the foundational chromosome of the Amte legend. Every family member—and the vast armies of volunteers and journeymen who have walked the path with them—seems to have it in differing measure. It has been, or is being, played out across a hundred projects in places like Anandwan, Somnath, Yavatmal and the banks of the Narmada. It has sprung hospitals and schools and universities and communes and self-generated employment out of unrelenting jungle and hard stone. Furthermore, it has sprung dignity and self-reliance for thousands of the most outcast and destitute. This simple, unassuming compassion—this way of life—presents itself as an unspoken challenge to the most fleeting of visitors.

The walk to the river is done, a light drizzle has set in. As the Amtes turn into their compound, a Madia family is leaving the hospital with a newborn baby, barely a few hours old. The mother, a frail slip of a girl, steps into the drizzle with her baby and climbs into a makeshift cart—a charpoy balanced between two bicycles. Simple, **stoic**, they walk into the rain. The OPD has begun. Lines of ailing tribal men and women walk to a counter and give their name and village; assistants either pull out old case histories **meticulously** filed, or make fresh ones. Diganth, now a qualified surgeon, and his wife Anika Sadhale, a gynecologist from Goa who laughingly says she did not just 'reply' to the matrimonial, she 'applied' for it, are at their stations—the third generation of Amtes to subsume their lives to the service of others. A severely **wheezing** barebreasted woman is slowly stopping to gasp. She had just raced past us at the river, perched on a motorcycle between two men. Now the generator has been put on, a nebulizer is breathing gentle breath into her. In the open air shed a short distance away, Prakash and Manda dress an amputated foot. The patient—an old man—lies stoically on the hard floor; he does not want a hospital bed. A wood-fire **smoulders** near him. A few feet away, a **ragged** skeleton is recovering from tuberculosis next to a toddler with kidney failure.

All of this would make an urban doctor faint, but in truth, it speaks of daily miracles over three decades. It speaks of lives saved without elaborate investigations or **prophylactics**. It speaks of urgent operations under torchlight, of emergency deliveries and complicated cataracts executed on the run with a textbook on the side. (Dr Prakash's first delivery was an emergency caesarean: a tranverse baby dead in the womb, a mother in shock. He had to literally cut the baby limb by limb out of the mother's body one night without anaesthesia in candlelight. She walked away the next day. A couple of years later, she returned to deliver a healthy child, alleviating some of the tortured dilemmas of that night.)

As the day progresses at Hemalkasa, 17 teachers in starched white and rows of boys and girls freshly fed in batches line up under some trees. A melodious song rises in the air to the resounding beat of a drum. The school has begun. When you remember that this project began with one teacher and 25 children of all ages, 15 of whom ran away in the first month, the standard issue buildings lose all of their disappointment. Hemalkasa is nothing short of a miracle wrought by human will.

Prakash—on the surface a mild, likable man, gifted with sudden bouts of delightful, self-deprecatory humour—is now taking a round of his orphanage, a menagerie of rescued animals brought in from the forests by tribals. Jaspar, the hyena, frolics with him, George Bush, the wolf, pounces on a roti and Ranghu, the leopard, playfully nibbles at his arm. Sheer spectacle, yet Prakash seems **disarmingly** untouched by his **accomplishments**. There is nothing pious or self-righteous about either him or Manda—what you get instead is an **infectious appetite** for adventure, a rich story told more in its physical evidence than in words. As Prakash moves from animal cage to patient, dressed in his perennial white vest and white shorts, little Arunav, their three-year old grandson, trails barefoot behind him, feeding the deer and squirrels, unconsciously absorbing his grandfather's fearlessness.

Prakash Amte and his son Diganth reduce a fracture in an old woman's wrist without any painkiller. The Madias' tolerance for pain is humbling. Life in Hemalkasa has always meant a continuous and present danger. A fraught tightrope between Naxal guns and state suspicion, nearfatal accidents and **bouts** of ill-health. Four years ago, while showing a poisonous Russel's viper to a visitor, Prakash was momentarily distracted and it emptied its fangs into him. But nothing can **perturb** him, his children **vouch**—he always exudes a quiet, **unflappable** dignity in a crisis. He is the shade tree you take for granted, until it is cut down. Now, instead of flinging the snake from him, he gently **extricated** it and put it back in its cage before walking towards Manda in the clinic. She, always the fit partner, the shadow he leans on, did not panic either. On his way back to the house while she got the antidote ready, Prakash collapsed at the threshold and his blood pressure dropped to zero. A long hot drive took him to Nagpur; 10 excruciating days followed. His body swelled like a balloon, blistering in a hundred places. Not once did he complain. Both husband and wife—still visibly and palpably in love—have this understated sturdiness about them. Not for them the glib sentence, the worldly pitch. Instead, you sense the close workings of Nature in them, a kind of wise acceptance born of daily grappling with life and death.

'One good thing came of the snake bite', Gopal Phadnis, headmaster and cotraveller at Hemalkasa, laughs. 'Prakash was never a talker, but he began to talk more after the bite'.

In faraway Anandwan, Prakash's 82-year old mother Sadhnatai says, 'I have no words to describe what Prakash and Manda have done. I feel guilty to think that they relived everything we had already been through, but I don't regret it once'. Tai's remembrance bears within it a vast and complex history. A double helix of sacrifice, a double helix of achievement.

It was not easy to be Baba and Tai's sons. Baba was a tall, tempestuous man, 'a living storm,' as Tai puts it, that came to roost in her nest. In trying to tame it, she became a part of the storm herself, as did her sons. Stories of Baba's youth abound. His family had ancestral homes and 450 acres of land, he wore pinstriped suits, hunted, played bridge and jazzed about in a Singer sports car nicknamed Green Lady with leopard skin covers on its seats. But very quickly things began to wreak transformations within him: there was Gandhi, Tagore, visits to Shantiniketan, Vinoba Bhave and the revolutionary poetry of Sane Guruji. There was also his growing sense of a wilful callousness in families like his, an engineered blindness to those less fortunate. But in a curious way, his mentally ill mother Laxmibai wrought the most powerful transformations. Her illness set her free from convention and, in turn, liberated her intensely loved son. 'I am basically the mad son of a mad mother', he once told a biographer.

That madness—creative, white hot—sent him on a frenzied journey that would last more than 70 years and draw thousands into its magnetic field. At first it led him through a series of purificatory experiments: he declared sanyas, grew his beard and nails and restricted his diet. But an accidental encounter with Sadhanatai, the shy daughter of a Brahmin family, put a quick end to that. An electric love blossomed. Tougher experiments followed. After their marriage, for instance, Baba took Tai, who had never crossed the boundaries of religion, community and caste, to live in Shram Ashram, a low-caste workers' commune in Warora. He followed this with stints as the president of the Sweepers' Union, and then as a night soil worker, cleaning dry latrines.

But all of this paled before Baba's chance meeting with a dying leper one dark, rainy night. If compassion is the X chromosome of the Amte legend, the Y chromosome is the confrontation of fear. Here was a man liquefying in maggots. Terrified, Baba—who prided himself on an absence of fear—recoiled physically. That image and his own fear plagued him so intensely, he forced himself to go back and tend to the man: Tulshiram. It became the pivotal experience of his life.

Training himself in the treatment of leprosy in the School of Tropical Medicine in Calcutta, in 1951, Baba moved with Tai and his toddler sons, Vikas and Prakash, to a grant land of 50 acres near Warora. Rocky, overrun by snakes and scorpions, it was, in his words, 'outcast land for outcast people'. Accompanied by six leprosy patients, one lame cow, one dog, Rs 14, and a comet's tail of stigma, they set up home under a bargat tree. Their horrified families did not visit them for over 10 years. Early life in Anandwan was a 'daily fight with death' as Sadhnatai puts it. There was heat, hard labour, leopards, scorpions, snakes, wild boar and a wild dream. The toddlers scratched about in the sand and played with the lepers' kids, while their parents worked. 'I could not even buy them a packet of biscuits for 50 annas', Tai remembers. 'I was so overworked, I used to get annoyed sometimes if they finished the dry rotis I packed for them in the morning. When Vikas was about five, he once came and asked me for some money. "What do you want it for", I asked him. He told me he wanted to go to the market and buy some friends'.

History is strewn with the tragic tailends of visionary men—**resentful** children who grow up hostile to their parents' legacy, sometimes **rebellious**, sometimes wasted, sometimes ordinary, inevitably nagged by a poor sense of self-worth. The

Amte boys could easily have gone that route. By all accounts, Baba was not the most simple of men—as father, husband or leader. A poet. A dreamer. A magnet. A soldier. **Hypnotic**. Heroic. **Eloquent**. **Inspirational**. **Quick-tempered**. Brusque. Impatient. Attributes flow around him in **kaleidoscopic** waves. 'It is difficult to understand Baba unless you met him. To talk of him now is like the story of the six blind men describing an elephant', **chuckles** Vilas Manohar, Prakash's brother-in-law and one of his staunchest allies in Hemalkasa. Vilas used to run a successful aircooler business and was a glider pilot and national rifle champion when he strayed into Baba's energy field during one of his famed youth camps at Somnath. 'I went to Anandwan and offered Baba some money. "More than money we need people", Baba said to me'. Moved, like scores of others, Vilas gave up everything. 'One way of understanding Baba', he says, 'is to trace the stories and observe the people who were drawn to him'.

But as with every Amte undertaking—beyond the words, beyond even the people, the work stands awesome **testimony**.

Vocabulary

1. **Clusters:** Bunch, group
2. **Emerald:** Bright green
3. **Wiry:** Thin, unbending
4. **Thronging:** Crowding, swarming
5. **Swirling:** Spinning, churning
6. **Indigenous:** Native, local
7. **Conventional:** Conservative, conformist
8. **Unorthodox:** Untraditional, unusual
9. **Lustrous:** Glistening, shiny
10. **Utter isolation:** Complete separation,
11. **Herculean:** Heroic formidable
12. **Compassion:** Kindness, consideration
13. **Gratification:** Satisfaction, fulfillment
14. **Meticulously:** Carefully, painstakingly
15. **Stoic:** A person who remains balanced in pleasure and pains
16. **Wheezing:** Out of breath, panting
17. **Prophylactics:** A medicine or course of action used to prevent disease
18. **Ragged:** Torn, worn out
19. **Smoulders:** Burns
20. **Disarmingly:** Charmingly
21. **Accomplishments:** Achievements, success
22. **Infectious appetite:** Contagious enthusiasm or eagerness
23. **Extricated:** Removed, disentangled
24. **Perturb:** Trouble, worry
25. **Bouts:** Sessions
26. **Unflappable:** Calm and composed
27. **Vouch:** Promise, guarantee

28. **Resentful:** Angry, indignant
29. **Rebellious:** Unruly, defiant
30. **Hypnotic:** Mesmerizing
31. **Eloquent:** Powerful, expressive
32. **Inspirational:** Inspiring, moving
33. **Kaleidoscopic:** Variety
34. **Chuckles:** Laughs gently
35. **Quick-tempered:** Passionate
36. **Testimony:** Proof, evidence

Reading Comprehension

1. Who are the quiet soldiers of compassion referred to in the passage? Why have they been called so?
2. What do we generally find in the forested heart of India 360 km from Nagpur?
3. Which award did Prakash and his wife receive? At what age? Why?
4. How did life begin at Hemalkasa? What was their usual diet? Which tribe belonged to this place?
5. What changes have taken place in Hemalkasa due to the efforts of Dr Prakash and Mandakini?
6. How did Prakash and his wife feel when their children failed in board exams? What kept them in Hemalkasa through all the frustrations?
7. What did Amte legend get by serving others? What have the banks of the Narmada spring due to their efforts?
8. What would make an urban doctor faint?
9. What did Prakash and his wife share?
10. 'I am basically the mad son of a mad mother'. Why did Prakash say these words to his biographer?

Language: Adjective and Adverb

Adjective

Study the following expressions from the text:
Note that all the highlighted words are adjectives.

Giant mosquitoes; **red**-verandah house; **40,000** Madia tribals; **None** of this; baby, barely **a few** hours old.

Adjectives are the describing words. They modify a *noun* or a *pronoun*, give more information and observation about it, describe its color, material, shape, size, amount, price, quality, origin, personality, weight, temperature, age, direction, etc.

Classification of Adjectives

There are mainly *six* types of adjectives:

- **Numeric:** six, one, hundred, first, second, several
- **Quantitative:** more, all, some, half, much, less, little, some, enough, great
- **Qualitative:** colour, size, smell, weary, worn, etc.
- **Distributive:** each, every, either, neither
- **Interrogative:** which, whose, what
- **Demonstrative:** this, that, those, these, yonder

Degrees of Comparison

There are three degrees of comparison: positive, comparative and superlative.

Positive Degree Is Used:

- To talk about one person or object: He is a good boy. This is a useful book.
- To show equality using 'as–as': That book is as expensive as the other one.
- To show comparison between two actions: Walking is as difficult as running in this weather. It is as difficult to read as to write in dim light.

Comparative Degree Is Used:

- To compare one object or person with another using 'than': He is wiser than his sister.
- To show parallel increase or decrease using 'the': The higher you go the colder it gets.

Superlative Degree Is Used:

- To express the highest degree of something or someone using the + superlative + of/ in:

  She is the most beautiful girl of/ in her class.

Exercise

Correct the following sentences:

1. No less than 60 students attended the class.
2. Tea is more preferable than coffee.
3. He is the oldest of my uncle's 3 sons.
4. He is so cunning as his sister.
5. She is weaker than any girl in the class.
6. She is comparatively weaker in English.
7. We met him prior than his departure.

Pronunciation

Compare the pronunciation of the pairs of words given below:

access/excess	accede/exceed	antic/antique
assay/essay	bed/bade/bad	belief/believe
bought/brought	bridal/bridle	defy/deify
device/devise	conform/confirm	disease/decease

Writing

As a nurse, which qualities of Baba Amte would you like to imbibe to make yourself professionally efficient?

10 The Story of a Caribbean Nurse

Trinidad, as you know, is the width and the length of the Atlantic Ocean away from Europe. But what we called 'the war in Europe' brought enemy activity from all over the world. Trinidad was then a British **colony** and loyal to the British crown, so England's war was also our war.

We were not bombed; we were short of some food but had plenty of others. We had few clothes in the shops. When I went to New York, right after the War in November, I had only a pair of sandals to wear—but I bought shoes in New York!

Great Britain had not made plans for a war, but the Germans had for a long time. They had spies positioned all over the world to keep them well-informed from early on. Trinidad, which was always a mixture of all races of people, was full of spies. I knew one or two at our Country Club and around the place, before they were **apprehended** and removed!

The Germans had filtered submarines throughout the south Atlantic as well as the north. They were our principal anxiety. The Island was full of servicemen. We had a Fleet Air Arm Station (the flying branch of the Navy) teaching young men to be Navigators. You may know that the smaller aircraft were **catapulted** off the warships. Attached to this station was a lovely small vessel, H.M.S. 'Corsair', used at sea as a practice target. I have forgotten the name of the type of aircraft at that station but I could always recognize their particular **drone** overhead.

Then there was another station, H.M.S. 'Benbow', for the officers and crews of a large fleet of Motor Torpedo Boats ('M.T.Bs'). I danced with many of those officers! The Americans had a complex building of offices for their administration. They took over **patrolling** the seas around the island seeking out submarines. They also had small 'look-out' stations on the coasts and points of Trinidad. They also had an enormous permanent camp for the aircraft that went on patrol and all sorts of personnel.

At one of our popular bathing bays, a U.S. naval base was set up which was unseen to us but was very large. After the war, they stayed on and used it to launch the early trial of unmanned satellites. We were allowed access to the beach on a separate path (the Americans swam on the other side) and, in return for using our holiday area, they built us a beautiful club house on the hill. We were permitted to use it all throughout the war.

At first, I was not married, and a friend and I took a Red Cross First Aid Course, then a Nursing Course. We were very keen to get high marks. My first volunteer job was to visit a huge temporarily arranged ward of English sailors and cheer them up. Their ship had been sunk off Africa and they had saved one lifeboat full of men whilst the others held on outside or were tied on. They were attacked by dogfish (a kind of shark) and could only splash and kick to protect them. They managed to pick up a floating old raft and towed so that everybody alive had a rest of sorts. The sun burned down on them and by the time they ended up in Trinidad they only had a little rain water left. If you look at an Atlas, you can see how many, many miles those men travelled and survived. They were amongst hundreds of other such cases.

Wally had his own small office in Port of Spain near the harbour, and Trinidad Leasehold Limited set him up with staff. He was responsible for arranging the collection of shipping that sailed out of Trinidad in convoy to protect each other. He also controlled the limited fuel oil supplies that had to be rationed out, considering the distance the ship had to travel before its next destination. No sooner had the convoy gone out, without fail one or two vessels were sunk and back came the survivors. Wally saw these men into specially set aside buildings to house them. Some poor men came back three and four times.

My next job was to serve a hot meal to the Maltese crew of the sunk ship. They could not speak English but were so polite and grateful. Then I had a severe bout of malaria and went to bed for weeks!

I saw a ship sink. I was on holiday with friends on the north coast. The house we were in looked across the sea from a cliff. My friend and I went swimming. We were quite alone; long white sands and a clear blue sea. We could look across to the island of Tobago. It looked so near and beautiful. We went back to the house to dress, leaving a lone cargo ship on the horizon, coming between Tobago and us. Sometimes, they did this and joined the convoy at the end of the Channel.

After my shower, I went to hang the wet bathing suits in the verandah and the same ship, as I was watching, had its **bow** thrown up high above the sea and then its **stern** came up the same way at the opposite end. It had broken in half in the middle. Those in the engine room would have been killed instantly. Later on in the evening, we saw the survivors (they were Greek) waiting in the school room for a bus and the big life boat was tied to the little wooden jetty. Whilst Helen (my friend) and I had been swimming we were sharing the clear blue sea with a German submarine close by. In Port of Spain there was also an enormous office block housing the **censorship** staff who were mostly young women and spoke several languages.

Then we got married and after that Wally did more volunteer work for the Red Cross and the other bodies and worked for wartime charities.

Vocabulary

1. **Colony:** A settlement; (here) a territory that has a foreign sovereign. During the First World War, India was a British colony.
2. **Apprehended:** Arrested ahead of committing a crime
3. **Catapulted:** Launched off aircraft carriers
4. **Drone:** An indistinct monotonous sound of a bee or a machine; buzz
5. **Patrolling:** Guarding a place by being on the move around the site
6. **Bow:** The front section of a boat or ship
7. **Stern:** The rear part of a ship or boat
8. **Censorship:** The act of screening texts and broadcast material to rule out the possibility of publishing something that goes against established laws.

Reading Comprehension

1. Why did Trinidad participate in the World War?
2. How far is Trinidad from Europe?
3. Why were the Germans ahead of the British in terms of war plans?
4. Describe the American efforts in the Caribbean.
5. Which part of the text tells us that the Americans were allies of the British?
6. Describe the plight of the group of patients that the author first attended to.

Language: Subject–verb Agreement

Study the following sentences:

- The **island was** full of servicemen.
- **Trinidad,** which was always a mixture of all races of people, **was** full of spies.

In the first sentence, the singular verb **'was'** agrees with its singular subject **'The island'**.

In the second sentence, the singular verb **'was'** agrees with its singular subject **'Trinidad',** although they are separated by **'which was always a mixture of all races of people'**. So you can observe that a verb always agrees with its subject. The verb must agree with the subject in number and person. The basic principle is: singular subjects need singular verbs; plural subjects need plural verbs. For example:

- My **brother is** a doctor.
- My **sisters are** teachers.

Study some of the important guidelines of subject-verb agreement:

1. Two or more singular subjects joined by 'and' take a plural verb:

   - *Oil* and *water do* not mix.

- A *car* and a *bike are* the popular means of transportation.

2. If two singular subjects are joined with—'as well as', 'in addition to', 'besides', 'not', 'with', 'along with', 'together with'—the verb agrees with the first subject:

- The owner *as well as* his servants *is* honest.
- Diseases *in addition to* poverty and illiteracy *pose* a big challenge in slums.
- You *not he have* been fined.
- The teacher *with/along with* his students *was* present in the programme.
- The leader *together with* his friends *is* going to prison.

3. When two subjects are joined with 'not only—but also' the verb agrees with the latter subject:

- *Not only* the students *but also* the teacher *was* asked to give a presentation.
- *Not only* the master *but* also his attendants *were also* praised.

4. Two singular subjects connected with—'or', 'nor', 'either–or', 'neither–nor'—take a singular verb. For example:

- *Neither* Joy nor Sam *is* available.
- Either Vandana or Jyoti is helping today with stage decorations.

5. The expressions, 'many a', 'a great deal of', 'one of the + (plural noun)', 'the number of', 'a majority of', 'pair of' take a singular verb:

- A *great deal of* patience *is* required to do this job.
- *One of the* boys *has* broken the flask.
- *The number of* books on this subject *is* very small.

6. The pronouns, 'anyone', 'anybody', 'everyone', 'everybody', 'someone', 'no one', 'nobody', 'each', 'every', 'neither', and 'either', are singular and take a singular verb:

- *Does anyone* else *want* to come?
- *Everybody has done* his or her homework.
- *Someone has left* her book.
- *Each of* these shops *is doing* good business.
- *Every* boy and *every* girl *was given* a sweet.

7. Adjectives—'much', 'less', 'little',—are used with uncountable nouns and take a singular verb:

- *Much* of the work *has been done*.
- It *is less* of a problem than I had expected.
- A *little* knowledge *is* a dangerous thing.

Exercise

Correct the following sentences:

1. This is one of the most difficult papers that has ever been set.
2. I am one who have always prayed for your well being.
3. Not only boys but their teacher also deserve praise.
4. Each of the suspected men was arrested.
5. A pair of spectacles are lying on the table.

Pronunciation

Practise the following tongue twisters loudly and rapidly:

1. I saw Susie sitting in a shoe shine shop.
2. Send toast to ten tense stout saints' ten tall tents.
3. Sheena leads, Sheila needs.
4. Stupid superstition!
5. Seventy seven benevolent elephants.
6. I scream, you scream, we all scream for ice-cream!
7. Thirty-three thirsty, thundering thoroughbreds thumped Mr. Thurber on Thursday.
8. Black background, brown background.
9. Green glass globes glow greenly.
10. I wish to wash my Irish wristwatch.

Writing

Study the life of the celebrated English nurse, Florence Nightingale, who came to prominence for her pioneering work in nursing during the Crimean War, where she looked after the wounded soldiers. Narrate an incident from her life that shows her unbound commitment to her profession.

Appendix 1: Group Discussion

As you graduate from college and take job interviews, you will be frequently asked to participate in group discussions. In most of our professional lives, group discussion is an important tool to help organizations arrive at crucial decisions. GDs, as they are called, help you to develop critical thinking skills, persuasion and negotiation skills, teamwork and interpersonal communication. In this chapter, we will focus on group discussions as a part of a job selection process, and will train you to take leadership roles in them.

Free discussion is the very life of truth.
—Thomas Huxley

The Use of Persuasive Strategies in a GD

A group discussion is all about a group of individuals sitting around a table to discuss an issue, a topic, a problem or a situation. In selection processes, group discussions are conducted to understand the ability of a candidate to communicate in a group effectively and assertively, the candidate's ability to find multiple solutions to the given situation if the topic is a problem-oriented one, or analyse the case logically if the topic is a case study. The selection bodies believe in informing the candidates about their rules, but a few of them do not care about it. If they explain the rules, you are supposed to follow them carefully. Otherwise, you should (as a group) decide whether you are going to follow a structured group discussion model, where each participant is given a chance to speak or an unstructured one where anyone can participate at any time and members of the group need not follow a rigid sequence. Then you should decide on how much time you are going to take (approximately). In the process of discussion, you are understood and evaluated as an individual and as a team. Coming to the skills, the panels evaluates listening skills, speaking skills, analytical and problem solving skills, leadership skills, and interpersonal skills:

To make a group discussion successful, it is important to pay attention to the following points:

Content

To make an impact in a group discussion, it is important to have good knowledge of the topic given. You should have a fairly good general knowledge and awareness of the current affairs. This will prevent ideas from drying up fast and keep the discussion alive and lively. If you are entirely unfamiliar with the topic given, wait for someone else to come up with important information and facts. Then quickly formulate your stance and come in with your perspective.

How can you improve your general knowledge?

- It always helps to know some major points about what is happening in the fields of the environment, gender, politics, sports, inventions and discoveries, wildlife, the arts and culture.
- Read the English newspapers carefully, especially the headlines.
- Listen to the news in English.
- Read weekly current affairs magazines such as *India Today, Outlook, The Week, Tehelka*, which provide political and cultural news in a nutshell.
- Always focus on the opinion pages of newspapers and magazines and watch talks and debates on TV news channels. This will give you ideas about framing arguments and getting perspectives on issues.
- Write down your opinions on whatever current event interests you. It will help you think critically.

Communication

Along with the knowledge of content, it is very important to know how you can communicate them effectively. It always helps to have a good grasp of vocabulary and fluency of speech. Using the right word at the right time gives clarity to the discussion and also highlights your role in generating ideas in the group. Again, remember not to exhaust your ideas at one go. Every time you contribute, make your talk brief and relevant. It is better to break into the discussion with a new idea each time rather than exhausting all your points the first time itself.

As most of the GDs today are carried out in English, you should possess good communication skills in English that will help you speak confidently and express your views convincingly. Remember, during the discussion your speaking skills are judged minutely. Adopt the following strategies to attain effective speaking and fluency:

- Use simple and appropriate words with the right pronunciation.
- Use grammatically correct sentences, concise and unambiguous expressions.
- Use simple language without exaggeration and flowery expressions.
- Speak fluently but with a moderate speed, pauses and volume.
- Use tone variation and do not let your speech become monotonous. Your tone should be pleasing and not commanding.
- Do not interact just in monosyllables such as 'yes' or 'no'.
- Do not use non-word fillers such as 'you know', 'you see', 'like', 'well,' etc., too often.
- Filler-sounds like 'aaaaaa.....', 'eeerrr' and 'ummmm.....' must be checked.
- A GD is an official interaction, so do not use slang.

- Use linking phrases to link arguments. 'Therefore', 'because', 'and so', 'thus', etc., are linking words.
- Make use of polite expressions to disagree or to interrupt others.
- Avoid using technical terms. Explain complex concepts in simple language.

Draw upon what you've learnt in the previous chapters to improve your communication skills and persuasive powers in a GD

- Reading: Reading is an important tool in preparing for a GD.
- Listening: Listening is integral in a GD. You must listen carefully to what your co-participants are saying, and how they are saying it, in order to respond to them (and counter them if necessary) effectively.
- Speaking: It goes without saying that speaking correctly, fluently and confidently will significantly improve your chances of being heard.

Critical Thinking

Critical thinking is one of the important activities during a group discussion. During a discussion you have to listen to and understand the arguments of the other participants and at the same time decide what points you should raise and how. A good discussion always involves a lot of networking. And networking involves active thinking, building on one another's points, negotiating, persuading and collating views.

Strategies to improve critical thinking

Developing critical thinking skills involves the following:

- **Restraining your emotions:** If you feel your emotions make you less objective (for example, you dislike someone in the group and therefore pay less attention to what they're saying, even if it is important), you need to consciously identify which emotions are responsible for this. Close your mind to the person and listen to the arguments. Listen to all sides of an argument before making up your mind. If you've already decided what you think at the beginning, your mind is going to be closed to other points of view. Try to understand why others think their point is valid. Try to recognize when you feel an increased heart-rate or when you're getting angry, and consciously calm yourself down by taking deep breaths.
- **Looking at things differently:** You need to learn how to look at an issue from many different angles. Try this with a current political or social issue. Write down points in favour of and against the issue. Think about long-term, short-term and immediate effects of an event if it was resolved in a particular way.
- **Analysing information:** Critical thinking goes further than thinking on a different or higher level or using emotional restraint; it also involves analysing information. To analyse, you need to break up a topic, statement, or problem, into parts to understand it well. Create a chart of the information using two columns. For example, take the issue of the death penalty. An analysis prevents you from poor answers like: 'It's good', or 'It's bad'. Instead, you are forced to ask why it is good

or bad. Connect your experience, newspaper reports and Internet information to form arguments.

- **Asking questions:** Curiosity is one of the most important traits that help us learn new things. Always ask questions that help you to learn. For example, if you could meet anyone on earth, whom would you meet and why? What questions would you ask him/her? Sometimes, you want to ask questions of experts or those whose opinions you value. What are the questions you will ask if you meet Manmohan Singh or Sachin Tendulkar?
- **Solving problems:** Many people don't know how to solve problems at work, home, or school. There are many ways to address issues and solve problems. The first thing to do is to identify the problem. For example, you are way behind schedule in preparing for your physics test and you haven't completed another assignment you were given. Is this the problem? Once you examine the situation closely, you realize that you have spent too many late nights with friends, and so had little sleep, were tired in the morning, and so could not concentrate on your work. So the real problem is not that you can't study well for the physics test or can't finish the assignment; the problem is that your social life is interfering with your work.

Then you need to gather ideas on different ways to solve your problem through brainstorming, or discussion with others. Note all the points and take the logical, unemotional, and practical solutions.

Knowledge of Group Dynamics

Employers today search for self-motivated candidates who can work in a team-oriented environment. So, group-management skills are a must for the participants of a GD. Organizers test you on whether you can get along with other people or whether you are a self-obsessed person. For this reason, participants have to understand that in a GD they will all succeed or fail together. If a member is not contributing, he/she will not only hurt himself/herself but also the group as a whole. You can manage a group well by using the following tactics:

- Generate agreement on a common viewpoint, which every member should work towards.
- Be adaptable and adjust with the other members.
- Show positive attitude towards others' views even if you do not agree with them.
- Do not indulge in needless talk or engage in private dialogue with your neighbour as it may distract others.
- Accept criticism sportingly.
- Motivate other participants to contribute and be cooperative.
- Deal with hostile members and conflicts tactfully; otherwise, the whole team will stand to lose.
- To join the discussion, drive yourself in at the earliest suitable moment of a pause: when a speaker has completed his/her argument; when a speaker is needlessly prolonging the argument; when the discussion is in a state of confusion and chaos; when you find a weak speaker unable to contribute.
- Never enter the discussion with a disagreement. First agree with the speaker and then present your views.

- Do not make personal remarks or show anger.
- Have a shared leadership as there is no elected leader in a GD.

The Process of a GD

Prior to the study of the methodology and the various components of a GD, let us first understand how a message flows in a GD:

1. A topic is declared beforehand, or a group is asked to choose a topic from the given ones. Participants may get 2 to 5 minutes to think.
2. In the usual format, anyone may initiate the discussion but a particular candidate may also be asked to express his/her views in brief, and others may follow him/her one by one so that the members get acquainted with one another's stands.
3. In the same way, any one of the members may come forward and conclude the GD or the participants may be asked to summarize it one by one.
4. The group may be asked to decide the procedure of the GD mutually or it may be given to them beforehand.
5. The discussion may take place on a topic to find a common solution to a given problem or a case study.
6. In the age of rapid advancement of communication technology, GDs can also be conducted through teleconferencing or video conferencing.
7. GDs may be conducted in the form of a case study where participants are given a case in writing. They study the topic carefully, think about its various aspects in 3 to 5 minutes, and then discuss it.

Topics for GDs

Abstract and Concrete

Topics given in group discussions can be broadly divided into two types:

1. Concrete and fact-oriented topics, which need factual content in combination with the right perspective to be successful.
2. Abstract topics where you need perceptive and creative thinking more than facts. Here, the perspective from which the interpretation is made and the themes you build into them will be more significant and valuable.

Group Work

Given below are some topics for group discussion. Divide them into the concrete and abstract types and see how many points you can build for each of them.

1. All the world is a stage.
2. Black is beautiful.
3. Deforestation is harmful.

4. Working mothers are better equipped to bring up children.
5. Marriages are made in heaven.
6. The ceiling is high.
7. Beauty lies in the beholder's eyes.
8. The sky is blue.

Make groups of six and discuss these topics for 20 minutes each.

Range of Topics

The range of topics for a GD is wide and a long list of topics can be prepared. However, we can roughly classify them for our convenience into **seven** categories as follows:

1. Current: Corruption is the price we pay for democracy/Cut-off marks for IIT entrance examinations should not be increased from 60 to 80 per cent.
2. Social: Euthanasia (mercy killing) should be legalized/Cricket is overemphasized in India.
3. Political: Value-based politics is the need of the hour/Women's reservation is the call of the day.
4. Economic: The current economic recession has not affected India's economy/The Sixth Pay Commission is a burden on the government.
5. Management: Women are better managers than men/The rush for MBA is really a rush for big money.
6. Abstract/creative: The wheel is turning round and round/When I woke up in the morning I saw....../A white dot/Blue grass.
7. Case studies: A swine flu case/Downfall of an XYZ company.

Structuring a GD

Here are a few language tips that will help you to structure a GD:

Opening: We're here today to discuss...
Let's decide how to proceed with the discussion.
Let's start with...
Can you please give your views on...?

Comments: What I think is...
I feel that...
The main point I wish to make is...
I agree up to a certain point but...
I must disagree with your opinion...
I would question whether...
It seems to me that...
As far as I'm concerned...

I don't agree with the previous speaker.
Please don't interrupt. Let me finish.
May I finish, please?
I think we are moving away from the main point.
If I may turn now to…
Turning now to…
I want to comment briefly on…
I intend to speak about…
Now, to elaborate on the first point…
I strongly believe that…
With all due respect…
I'm not in a position to say anything about…
If we look at it in another light…
On the contrary…
I don't think anyone could disagree with…
I can't help thinking…
Finally…

Leadership Skills

Employers look not only for team workers but also for leaders; so, in every GD they seek an element of leadership. They observe the participants very closely and pinpoint those who have good leadership traits. The success or failure of a GD depends a lot on the utilization of the elements of leadership. All GDs provide their participants with numerous opportunities to exhibit their leadership qualities as well as to steer the discussion to its success. Every member should try to be the first to grab the chance to show his/her leadership traits. In the sections below, we discuss various leadership traits.

Being Polite but Firm

In order to be a leader in a GD, you need to learn how to make your point politely but firmly. People often avoid being assertive because they think they will sound rude. But taking a stand, holding on to your arguments and not letting others bully you are signs of your self-confidence and will gain you respect from others. Being polite but firm essentially means that you want to win but you will not trample over others in order to do so. Here's how you can be more assertive in GDs:

- Don't apologize when you disagree with someone. Don't begin with 'I'm sorry but…' Apologize only when you've done something wrong.
- Don't make sentences sound like questions: If you raise your pitch at the end of the sentence, it'll sound like you're unsure of what you are saying. For example, notice the difference between 'We shall be going' and 'We shall be going?'
- Avoid using tag questions, like 'That's not fair, is it?' Such questions make you seem unsure of yourself. Just say, 'I don't think that's fair'.
- Don't say anything unless you've completed your thoughts; otherwise, you'll not know how to finish your arguments.

- Use the 'I' language, 'I think', 'I feel', especially to make negative comments. This is assertive but not rude. But never say 'You are': you'll be making accusations.
- Do not allow yourself to be interrupted unnecessarily. If someone keeps interrupting, you can say politely, but firmly, 'May I please finish?' or 'I wasn't finished.'
- To make a statement powerful, try and drop the tone of your voice at the end of the sentence. This minor change makes a major difference.

Handling Difficult Questions and Criticism

One of the trickiest things to manage is how to answer questions that are directed straight at you. How you handle questions and criticism shows your ability to manage people, conflicts and control a situation. Often, questions are simply asked to stump you, and you need to appear calm through them and not become nervous. When you are a leader you are going to be challenged and criticized.

Once in a while, a group will have a troublemaker who will criticize just to make others uncomfortable and lose focus. Remember that the others, too, will not like such a person. Sometimes the best way to deal with such people is to ignore them and when you do so, the others will also join you. If that person refuses to stop talking or making personal comments, the best way is to be coldly polite and suggest that everyone sticks to the discussion at hand. 'Do you have a point to make?' is a question—rude, but sometimes necessary for bullies—that works effectively.

Remember: The most important thing is to remain calm. Take deep breaths whenever you feel nervous or upset and try to focus on the points of the discussion.

Questions

- Before you answer a question, always think it over. Carefully hear what is being asked and then frame the response in your head. Ask yourself if the other person is simply asking a question to challenge you, or to know what you mean. Don't be in a hurry to respond. You can say: 'Let me get this clear: you are asking if …'
- Avoid prolonged discussions, responses and arguments with one person.
- Avoid providing detailed responses to questions that will take the focus away from the discussion at hand. Tell the person politely that you have noted the question but will take it up later. Be sure to do so. But if it directly relates to the point at hand, answer the question immediately.
- An important strategy is to pre-empt a difficult question. If you are watching your co-participants carefully, you'll know when they are about to ask you a difficult question. Developing your critical thinking skills will help you guess what questions might be asked and prepare answers to them before the GD.
- After you've responded to a person, ask them if you've answers to them them to their satisfaction.

Criticisms

How you handle criticism says a lot about you, and about who you think you are.

- The most important point is to not become nervous and defensive the moment someone disagrees with you or criticizes your views. Logically analyse the criticism: is the person attacking a flaw in your argument or is he/she disagreeing with the basic approach? If there is a flaw, quickly restate your argument, remedying the flaw. If the approach is being criticized, you need to clearly state why you have made that point, and cite data and figures to support your statement.
- Keep an open mind and try to judge your own statements objectively. If a person has made a valid point, thank them for making that point and try to fix your statements.
- Don't hold grudges against people: this will make you lose your focus and you'll begin to make mistakes—so be gracious.

Remember: If you are being criticized, it does not mean that there is something wrong with you. Handle criticism objectively and positively.

Exercises

Perform these mock GDs with your friends:

(a) Justice delayed is justice denied.
(b) Examinations should be abolished.
(c) Female foeticide is a crime against God.

Turn-taking and Effective Intervention Strategies

A successful GD is where everyone gets an equal chance to speak about the topic. When you are a part of a GD, ensure that no one person grabs the limelight and snubs the others. Do not talk continuously yourself: let others speak.

You will emerge as a true leader if you can turn the conversation in a way that others get a chance to speak too. Here are some tips to get you going:

- If you want everyone to have their turn, you need to ensure that you don't go on speaking yourself. Play fair and keep your arguments short and precise.
- Don't speak just to interrupt someone, but don't keep quiet if you have something to say and you find others already talking a lot.
- If you see someone trying to put in a word and not being successful, you can always intervene and say, 'I think [Name] has something to say.'
- If you need to make a point, you can say, 'I have something to add' or 'There are other ways to look at this point. For example ...' 'We also need to consider ...' You can say 'Excuse me' loudly to draw attention if there is too much noise and you can't be heard.
- If the GD becomes unfocused, you can intervene by saying, 'Let's stick to the point. We were discussing ...'

- If too many people are speaking at the same time, you can say, 'Let's make our points one after another, okay? [Name], why don't you start?

Here is an example of a GD that will give you a practical demonstration of all that we've discussed so far.

Example of a GD

Aditi, Bijoy, Charu, Daisy and Ehsan are waiting for their group discussion to start. They do not have a topic yet and are waiting for the moderator to make everybody comfortable. There, the moderator looks at the clock and announces: 'You have five minutes for this group discussion. And your topic is "How to Succeed in Group Discussions." Please start.'

Bijoy: This should be interesting. A GD on GD! I suggest we discuss the importance of a GD first. I mean, why have a GD at all?

Charu: I find this very strange. How can you have a GD on GD? We should be discussing some current topic to test our knowledge.

Ehsan: I agree that this is rather unusual. At the same time, our job is to conduct a meaningful discussion regardless of the topic. Bijoy has suggested we start with the importance of GD. Today, GD is a very important part of various selection procedures.

Aditi: GD is all about teamwork. That's all.

Bijoy: Management is all about working with people. I suppose GD is one way of establishing one's ability to work with others. How we are able to lead and be led.

Charu: (Laughs) You are using some impressive management jargon, my friend! I don't think a GD has anything to do with leading or being led. At the most, a GD may suggest ideas on how a business meeting is held. Otherwise, it is only about sharing your knowledge with others.

Bijoy: (Visibly irritated) Looks like you are very sure about your knowledge. Perhaps there is no need for a group or even a discussion?

Ehsan: We have some interesting points here—leadership and sharing knowledge. Perhaps a GD is a good tool to assess how well you are able to function within a group.

Daisy: I want to…

Aditi: I don't think any discussion is meaningful unless everyone has the same level of knowledge.

Daisy: I want to say something. Pardon if I make any wrong. I am from a regional medium…

Aditi: Don't waste our time talking about your background. The topic is GD. Talk about that.

Bijoy: Every subject has various angles. So, many heads can raise many ideas.

Charu: Also, too many cooks spoil the broth (laughs).

Ehsan: Yes, a group makes it possible to brainstorm any issue. Perhaps Daisy has something to add to this thought.

Daisy: Thanks for giving me chance. A GD is good for consense. It is always better if everybody agrees.

Charu: (Leaning forward and pointing to Daisy) I think the correct word is consensus. Don't use a word unless you know what you are talking about.

Bijoy: Consensus is fine. But is it necessary that everyone should have the same viewpoint?

Ehsan: That is an interesting thought. Yes, Daisy is right that a GD is about consensus but there can still be differences. A GD provides an opportunity to discuss various aspects of an issue and weigh the merits and demerits of different approaches.

Charu: I agree to disagree.

Bijoy: But the question is how to succeed in GDs. I think the first prerequisite is patience. Some of us must learn to shut up and let others talk (looks directly at Charu).

Aditi: If everyone follows that, we will only have silence and no discussion.

Ehsan: I suppose the point is to participate and give others a chance to participate as well.

Daisy: Please can I speak?

Aditi: Come on! You don't have to beg for permission to speak!

Daisy: I said that because I thought someone might have wanted to speak before me. Anyway, is it not possible to only listen?

Charu: (Smirks) I don't know how the moderator will rate your profound silence!

Bijoy: But Daisy, no one can read your mind. Unless you speak, how do you contribute?

Ehsan: I think a GD is very much like a business meeting. Every participant may present an individual point of view but thinking about that point of view is a collective effort.

Aditi: I don't think you can compare a GD to a business meeting. In a meeting, there is usually a chairman whose job is to control the meeting.

Bijoy: A GD may not have a chairman, but I suppose one person usually emerges as the leader and guides the discussion.

Charu: I suppose someone fancies himself a leader. This is so boring!

Moderator: Your time is up. Thank you, everyone.

Notes: *Ehsan shows leadership skills and the ability to hold a group together. He appears to have a good grasp of the subject though, on the whole, the GD failed to do justice to the core subject of how to succeed. Bijoy also has some interesting ideas but is prone to being provoked easily. Charu is too sure and too full of herself to be able to contribute to a group. Aditi is guilty of intolerance and rude interruptions. Daisy needs to work on her language and her confidence, though she may have the right concepts.*

Examiners are advised to arrange a group of 8 to 10 students around a table, announce the topic, and set the rules. Divide the rest of the students into a few groups and give them the parameters to examine the performing group. After the performance is complete, ask the peer groups to present their analyses. The teacher should also present his/her analysis. Then each performer should be asked to answer self-performance questions. Repeat this at least twice and notice the improvement.

The Use of Appropriate Body Language

Body language is a non-verbal communication signal that you, as a participant, transmit to the other members of the group. Your body cues help others judge your confidence, openness, composure, cooperativeness, friendliness, alertness, insecurity, nervousness, positive or negative attitude, and so forth. Remember that you should not be conscious of your non-verbal signals. 'Energetic outside but composed from within' is a mantra that can help you exhibit positive body language.

Some of the important non-verbal pointers that you should try to adopt are as follows.

Dress and Appearance

Dress and appearance matter a lot in creating a first impression about yourself even before you have spoken a single word. You should be careful about your dress as well as your looks. The following tips may help:

- Your dress should be sober, neat and well-stitched. It need not be costly, new or fashionable as newly acquired clothes can make you self-conscious, cause discomfort and affect your performance. A well-dressed participant feels confident.
- Your footwear should be formal, polished and clean. Men must make sure that their socks are drawn tightly up their legs, and not rolled down.
- Your hair should be cut neatly in a style that suits your personality and combed properly.
- Your nails should be clean and well-kept.
- Take care of personal hygiene, but don't wear an overpowering perfume that gives everyone a headache!
- Dark trousers, a light-coloured matching shirt with a sober tie is an ideal dress for men, while women may wear formal trousers and shirts or formal Indian attire. Avoid wearing jeans and a T-shirt.

Eye Contact

Eye contact is the most important of all non-verbal cues in group discussions. When you are speaking, you should remember that every member of the group is equally important, so give that impression to all the members. Make eye contact with each person in the group. When another participant is speaking, you are supposed to look straight into his/her eyes (but don't stare or make them uncomfortable). Maintaining an eye contact shows that you are listening attentively. Moreover, when you look in to the eyes of a speaker, there is always a chance that you can interrupt him if he is going overboard.

Facial Expressions

First and foremost, you need to remember that a GD is a formal forum and requires formal etiquette. Being polite is very important, and expressing that through facial expression is essential. Showing negative emotions like anger, irritation and frustration clearly sends alarming signals to the members, so avoid revealing them. Wear a pleasant, warm, confident and friendly facial expressions.

Hand Movements

It is not advisable to lean on the table or play with things on the table. You should use your hand appropriately while speaking to the audience. But when someone else is speaking, do not move hour hand unless it is very urgent. Don't touch the other participants. Don't put your hands in your pockets or sit with your hands crossed over your chest: these show defensiveness. Don't fiddle with things such as your pen, wristwatch, bangle, buttons, tie and hair. Above all, don't point your index finger at others while speaking, as such a gesture is considered rude.

Posture

Seat yourself comfortably and show assertion in your posture, that is, do not throw your body forward or be rigid. Relax your shoulders. Sit straight with your head held erect and do not lean on the table or the sides. Don't shake your legs or cross them.

Distance and Angles

Don't sit either too close or too far away from the person next to you. If you're sitting too close, you are seen as aggressive and if you're too far away, you will be seen as a cold and aloof person.

Voice Modulation

Pace

Speaking fast has two disadvantages. One, it blurs the clarity, and two, it puts unnecessary pressure on you. Speaking too slowly also has two disadvantages: A slow speech is boring to listen to, and there is a chance that you may lose the thread of your argument yourself. So, it is best to maintain optimum speed.

Pitch

Analyse the size of your group and that of the table, and speak in an audible and pleasant pitch. You should be heard clearly by all but you should not drown out everyone else's voice.

Tone

Tone refers to your approach and attitude towards the topic at hand, and is conveyed through your voice. The tone should be polite, pleasant and serious.

Pronunciation

Go through the section on pronunciation in Chapter 6. Don't 'eat up' syllables or words in a sentence. For example, when you say 'preparation', take the time to pronounce all the syllables, instead of saying 'prapration'.

Enunciation

Moderate speed, right pitch, appropriate tone, and intelligible pronunciation give clarity, i.e., correct enunciation to the speech. Thus, you should express self-confidence, optimism, sincerity, and a friendly personality through your verbal and non-verbal communication. While appearing before the group, remember that your first impression is extremely important and to make an effective first impression, being courteous, helpful, polite, well-dressed and assertive are very important.

Here's a quick look at the important do's and don'ts in a GD.

Do's	*Don'ts*
1. Seat yourself comfortably.	1. Be in a hurry to start discussing.
2. Listen to the topic carefully.	2. Be silent.
3. Organize your ideas before speaking.	3. Dominate vocally/physically.
4. Speak at the earliest opportunity.	4. Assume the role of the chairman.
5. Be polite.	5. Take an extreme stance.
6. Identify your supporters and opponents.	6. Enter into an argument.
7. Allow your supporters to finish their arguments.	7. Make value judgements.
8. Keep track of the time.	8. Look at the faculty.
9. Share time fairly.	9. Shout at inert participants.
10. Listen to others' points.	10. Move excessively in your chair or lean on the table.

Group Work

In groups of five, perform GDs on the topics listed below. There should be moderator who will jot down the major points of the discussion and evaluate the speakers. Ideally, teachers should take on this role.

1. Terror attacks on Indian cities.
2. The financial mess in the world.
3. Technical research and development in India at present.
4. Should charge sheeted politicians resign?
5. Glorification of violence and sex in media accounts.
6. Are strikes justifiable?
7. What is the place of literature in technical education in India?
8. Reservation poses a threat to national unity and integration.
9. Indian youth needs a realistic goal.
10. Science is universal but technology is local.

11. The necessity of building green buildings.
12. Technology after 20 years.
13. Clean technology is the need of the hour.
14. Reverse engineering and its importance.

Case Study

Distribute the following case among each of the participants. Think about the situation and discuss what, according to you, was right or wrong with Manish's and Subramanyam's individual behaviour. Try to find the response of others in the group and see if you can arrive at a consensus.

Answer these questions during the course of your discussion: What are the broader questions related to business ethics and personal values that are being asked here? Can you think of similar situations where corporate culture and personal values may clash? Which do you think should be followed?

When Manish received Subramanyam at the station, he was delighted to find him bright, cheerful and healthy. Manish is a senior HR manager in a pharmaceutical company. The company has been doing well for the last 10 years. He is happy with his job, and he finds it challenging and **invigorating**. He is stressed at times but he has accepted it as part of the profession. Apart from being an efficient HR manager, he is also a warm and friendly person who values relationships. Subramanyam is a former colleague of Manish. He, too, was in a fairly senior and comfortable position, working in the marketing division of the company. Subramanyam is a warm and friendly person as well, and is well liked by those around him. He is and reasonably successful in business too.

About a year back, Subramanyam had started feeling a growing sense of **dissatisfaction**. He was beginning to get **disillusioned** with the corporate culture. He detested the way in which selfish interests were being **ruthlessly** pursued and **self-aggrandizement** was celebrated and appreciated. Coming from a family of freedom fighters and social workers, he found himself feeling increasingly **suffocated** in the atmosphere of '**dog-eat-dog**' competition. Subramanyam is a person with a lot of creative talent and original thinking. At a time when his family needed money, this job had come as a godsent opportunity. Though not fascinated, Subramanyam was fairly happy and successful at work. But as the immediate need for money **dwindled**, he began seeing things differently. The unfairness of most of the deals, some of which were handled by him, made him very uneasy. He even began thinking that the work he was doing was **redundant**. 'It needs a bit of tact and a strategic mind to wrap products in layers of lies and sell them', he would say. 'But it needs a lifetime's dedication to bring about a slight change in the people's way of living.' He disliked the market, which bloodied people and crushed them to sell soaps or toothpastes or drugs that everyone knew were not as effective as they were proclaimed to be. Manish had tried his best to convince Subramanyam. 'You cannot run away from competition', he had said. 'It is a reality and you will have to accept it as such.' Manish had tried to make him see the positive features of industrialization. 'The lot of Indians also improves when foreign exchange comes in. We are a part of the global community and we'll have to abide by the rules of the game. Moreover, everything is fair in love and war', Manish would say. Manish had also suggested that Subramanyam be transferred to the urban development sector of their company. 'You will be in immediate touch with people, you can work for them and with them', he had told Subramanyam. But Subramanyam was bent on a complete changeover. Six months ago, Manish finally stopped trying to convince Subramanyam. Eventually, Subramanyam bought a plot of land on the outskirts of the city and started to set up an awareness centre that would provide information to the rural people about the different kinds themselves of facilities they can avail themselves of. Later, Subramanyam admitted his only son Lalit, who had two more years of schooling left, in the hostel of the same school and shifted out with his wife Sheela.

At the railway station, Manish asked, 'Happy now? Got what you wanted finally?' 'Oh yes!' a beaming Subramanyam replied. 'I make a decent living off my centre. Lalit comes home on weekends, sometimes **commutes** from home too. Sheela and he are delighted with their new house. They love spending more time with one another. Thank God I didn't listen to you. I have earned enough money. After all, one has to pamper oneself and one's family too!' he told Manish. Manish still believed differently. According to him, Subramanyam was chasing a rainbow, a dream. But for Subramanyam, the rainbow was firmly rooted in reality. It was something he felt and perceived every hour of his life.

ACTIVITIES

Word meanings:

commute: to travel regularly over a long distance to get to work.
disillusioned: to be disappointed at having lost one's belief in something that was previously considered good or right.
dissatisfaction: a feeling of not being satisfied.
dog-eat-dog: a situation in which people fight for themselves and hurt other people while pursuing their self-interest.
dwindl: to gradually become less and less.
invigorating: a feeling of rejuvenation due to generation of a lot of energy.
perceive: to think of something or someone in a particular way.
redundant: not necessary.
ruthlessly: to do something in a determined way such that one does not care if others get hurt.
self-aggrandizement: the act of increasing one's importance, power, etc.
suffocated: to feel as if one is not free or as if there isn't enough space.

Appendix 2: Written Communication

In the earlier chapters, you have learnt how to read, speak, listen and participate in discussions. Of all the skills you need to acquire, writing is the most difficult and complex. There are many things to take care of: from conceptualizing what you are going to write about and how you will go about it, to doing research, organizing the information, and writing it all down, and then editing and formatting your text for presentation. So before you even begin to write, you need to have a lot of things clear in your head about communication in general. We hope that whatever you've learnt in the previous chapters will help you to think and write better.

Note Taking and Note Making

Note Taking

Note taking is a method of writing down the crucial items of a lecture, a meeting or a reading text rapidly, briefly and clearly. Studies show that we tend to forget a good part of a lecture within 24 hours. Unless one has excellent memory, one should take notes for future reference. Whether you are a high-school student or a university scholar or a professional, the ability to take effective, meaningful and comprehensive notes is an important skill. Good notes save our study time as they help us review the text for reuse during test preparations, assignments and meetings. At the same time, taking notes helps us concentrate in class and facilitates a deeper understanding of a topic. Two major questions relate to note taking—what to write and how to write.

What to Write

While taking notes, only the most important parts of a lecture/text should be included. If you try to write down everything your professor is saying, you will not be able to keep up and after a while will lose track of the entire lecture. Listen or read carefully for key words/phrases and jot them down. Try to analyse the relations between points and write down any questions or comments that come to your mind.

Focus on the following:

1. What is new to you? There is no use in writing down facts you already know.
2. What is relevant? Focus on the points that are directly related to your reading material. The details on which you should pay special attention are—dates, numbers, titles, names of people and books, theories, concepts, definitions, arguments, diagrams, exercises, speaker's conclusion, comments of the other listeners as well as your own interpretation, doubts or questions. Examples, idiomatic expressions and minute details should be excluded.
3. Go to the listening chapter to recall the key words and phrases in a lecture to which you need to give extra attention.

How to Take Notes

Although note-taking techniques are specific to different people, you may use the following guidelines for effective note-taking:

1. **Outlining:** Outlining is an effective way to take notes in a hierarchical structure. You may use the alphabet, numbers, Roman numerals or bullets/dots to indicate the structure. Outlining can be very useful while taking notes from books and presentations because the authors usually organize the material in a fairly effective way. For lectures, however, outlining has some limitations. The speaker does not necessarily maintain connection between ideas, consequently, there is a risk of losing the relationship between what the speaker just said and what he/she said before.
2. **Mind Mapping:** For lectures, a mind mapping may be a better option to keep track of the connections between ideas. Write the main topic of the lecture in the centre of a blank sheet of paper. As a new subtopic is introduced, draw a branch outward from the centre and write the subtopic at the end of the branch (see Figure A.1). Then each point under that heading gets its own, smaller, branch off the main one. When another new subtopic is mentioned, draw a new main branch from the centre and so on. If a point is under the first heading but you are on the fourth one, you can easily draw it in on the first branch. Similarly, if a point connects to two different ideas, you can connect it to two different branches.
3. **The Cornell System:** The Cornell System is a simple but effective system of note taking. It was devised in the 1950s by Walter Pauk, professor of Education at Cornell University, New York. In this system, we have to leave about 3.5 inches space from the bottom of a sheet of paper and draw a line across the width of the page to mark this space. Draw another line from that line to the top, about 2.5 inches from the left-hand edge of the sheet.

Now you have divided your sheet into three sections, the largest section is the 'notes column'. Take down notes in this space—you can outline or mind map or whatever is suitable to you. Write legibly. The column on the left is the 'recall column', wherein you write a series of cues, hints or questions about the corresponding item you have just taken down in the notes. Now cover the 'notes column' and use the 'recall column' to help you remember facts, ideas and information of the lecture as completely as you can. Then, uncover your notes and verify what you have recalled. Then in the bottom section write a short, 2–3-line summary in your words of the notes you have taken down. This helps you process the information, provide a useful reference when you are trying to find something in your notes later and transfer facts and ideas to your long-term memory. Figure A.2 gives you the format of the 'The Cornell System' of note taking.

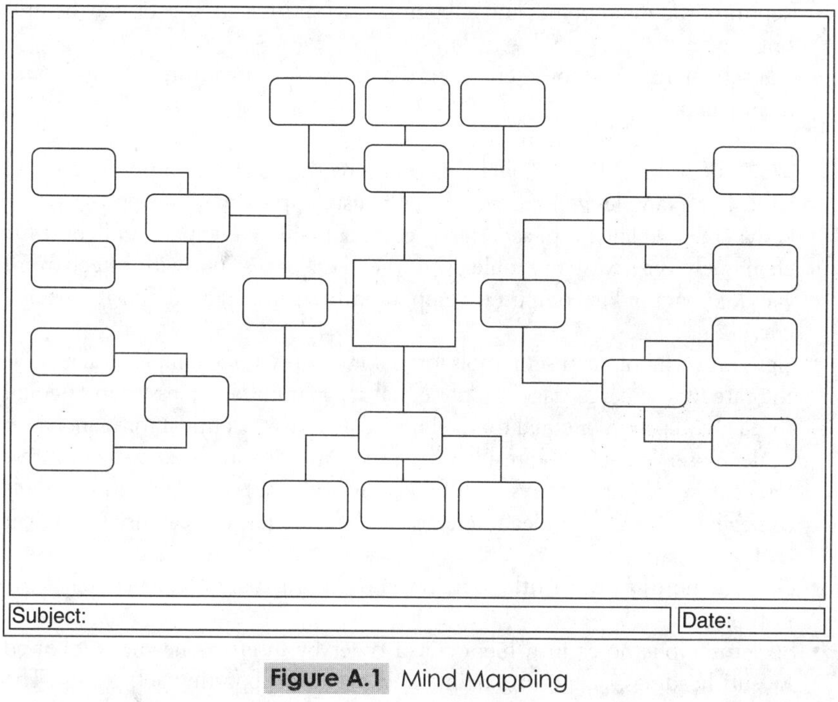

Figure A.1 Mind Mapping

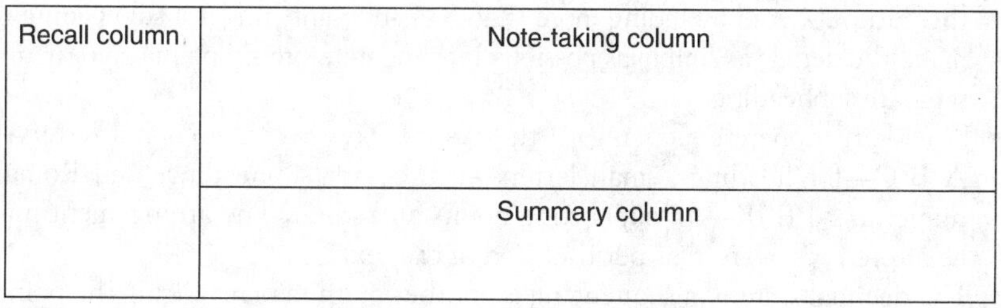

Figure A.2 The Cornell System

Making Notes from Text

Go back to the reading chapter and see what we had said about *comprehension*. One of the best ways to comprehend a text is to make notes while you're reading. Good notes will also help you a lot while preparing for your examinations, when you have to quickly read the main points. Here's how you can make the best notes:

- Skim the text briskly to grasp its gist, purpose and key points. At the same time, take notes.
- Read it again, this time more carefully, to find out the development of idea, the main divisions/chapters/sections of the text and their mutual relationships.
- Write down the main points and the subpoints in the order as they appear in the text.
- Rephrase the main points and subpoints into shorter phrases or may be into single words.
- Use schematizing—tables, charts or diagrams—for organizing scientific and technical material.
- Use standard abbreviations to save time. The first few letters of words and phrases can be the functional abbreviations that may be easily understood later. For example, volume: vol; usually: usu; approximately: approx; somebody: sb; especially: esp; secretary: secy; that is: i.e.; compare and contrast: cf; namely: viz; west: w; joule: J; oxygen: O; pages: pp; with effect from: w.e.f.; kilogram: kg; computer: comp; month: mth; magnesium: Mg; specific gravity: sg.
- Signs and symbols are useful tools for making notes. For example, dollar: $; at the rate of: @; percentage: %; not equal to: ≠; infinity: ∞; less than or equal to: ≤; greater than or equal to: ≥; almost equal to: ≈, identical to: ≡; increase: ↑; decrease: ↓; cause: →; results: ←; important: *; and: &, and so on. Don't forget to write out the keys with full forms of the abbreviations and symbols somewhere. It's a good idea to memorize them so that you can use them over and over again.
- Give the notes a proper title to help you recall the main theme as well as the gist.
- Structure your notes in a hierarchical order by inserting headings followed by sub headings, supporting points and may be supporting sub-points. The order of the headings should be logical so as to convey the right attitude of the author. Avoid including more than 3–4 subpoints under a subheading to make the details as simple as possible. If there are more subpoints give them a separate subheading.
- Provide a proper sequencing to the points. You may use capital letters—A B C—for headings, small letters—a b c—for subheadings and Roman numerals—I II III—for supporting points and so on. The arrangement may be altered or reversed as per the need of the text.
- The decimal system of sequencing is another method of arranging the points systematically. Study the following illustration:

1________________
    1.1________________
    1.2________________
        1.2.1________________
        1.2.2________________
2________________
    2.1________________
    2.2________________
        2.2.1________________
        2.2.2________________

- Write down your comments next to the main points of the notes. This will help you remember later what you were thinking

Passage 1: Making Notes

Read the follow passage carefully and make notes on it. Further, supply a suitable title to it.

A robot can be defined as a mechanical gadget that performs functions normally ascribed to human beings. Karel Capek introduced the word 'robot' while Sir Isaac Asimov coined the word 'robotics', which is a science of dealing with robots. The study of robotics includes the selection of material of proper quality for the components, design, fabrication, design of electronic circuits, computers and computer programming and its control. The science of robots is still in the development stage and a lot of research is being pursued to make robots more suitable for working. Depending upon the area in which robots are to be used, robotics is a multidimensional field that includes disciplines such as biology, medical science, psychology, agriculture, mining, various branches of engineering, outer space, etc. At present, robots are mainly used in industries. These industrial robots are reprogrammable and perform a variety of jobs through programmed motions. Basically, there are two types of robots: fixed and mobile. A fixed robot is attached to an immovable platform. It is similar to a human being standing or sitting in a fixed position while doing the work with hands. On the other hand, a mobile robot moves from place to place. The mobility of a robot is due to wheels or legs or other crawling material provided to it. A mobile robot can be given a human shape. However, the actual shape has nothing to do with the real functioning of the robot.

Summarizing

Summarizing is another effective tool that will help you to comprehend your text materials and write them better in your own words. *Summarizing essentially means that we reduce a text to its major points.* A good summary will give you a clear idea of what a chapter or article is about. Have you seen any scientific article? Many of them have what is called an 'abstract' at the beginning (see Figure A.3). Abstracts are similar to summaries, in the sense that they'll mention in brief what the main text discusses in detail. Some articles also have summaries at the end. Read some abstracts and summaries and see how the main points of the text have been summarized in them.

Abstract →

Liquid crystals (LCs) are known for the ubiquitous display (LCD) devices. Though liquid crystals were discovered in 1888 in Austria, the first Indian research work on the subject was reported only in the 1950s by Dave from Baroda, on the synthesis of new compounds. Chandrasekhar initiated the most comprehensive activity in the field in the 1960s in Mysore. The most important Indian contribution is the discovery of columnar liquid crystals made of disc-like molecules. Chandrasekhar also authored a well-cited book on liquid crystals. Over the past four decades, many other well-known theoretical as well as experimental contributions have been made, and over 1,000 papers have been published on the subject, from India. However, applied work in this field has been on a low key. An indigenous know-how for the manufacture of simple LCD devices was developed by a cooperation between the Raman Research Institute and Bharat Electronics Limited. The paper will cover the most important advances made by Indian scientists, using a semi-technical presentation.

INTRODUCTION

Main text →

Liquid crystals (LCs) are now seen practically by everyone. Or rather, we see many things because of liquid crystals. The time on the digital watch, the caller ID on the cellphone, the information about the volume and the price of petrol that one has filled up in the vehicle, the progress of this paper that I am writing using a laptop computer are all seen on liquid crystal displays or LCDs. These flat-panel

Figure A.3 Example of an Abstract

The two mistakes we usually make when we try to summarize something is, we either write down everything, and mostly copy the text word for word; or forget to write down the important points and write too little to be helpful. Making good summaries is difficult, but once you know how to do it, it will help you all your life to learn new things.

Underlining or Highlighting

What are the key ideas in a chapter or passage? Key words are usually marked out in textbooks in bold, and they indicate important points to remember. What are the points raised in each section? Where can you locate the answer in that section? In a well-written article, usually each large paragraph will have at least one important point. Read through paragraphs to identify the point it is making.

A great way to learn to highlight is to read a newspaper or magazine article and highlight only those lines that answer the questions: 'what', 'when', 'where', 'why' and 'how'. Once you get used to this, it will be easier to quickly read and highlight.

Jotting Down the Key Points

From the underlined or highlighted sections, now write down, *in your own words*, the main points of those sections. If a chapter has 2,000 words, your summary should at the most have 200 words. Start with reducing the size of the summary to 100 words, then to 50, and then as short as you can make it. Can you sum up one chapter in a single sentence?

Exercises

1. Imagine that you are putting in an ad, you have Rs 1,000 and you pay Rs 10 for every word you use. Now, go through a chapter you are reading and create a summary within your 'budget'.
2. In most interviews, you are asked to say something about yourself. Try this exercise:
   a) If you were to describe yourself in one sentence, how would you do it?
   b) If you had one last wish to make, what would it be?
   c) Name three books you really like. For each book, write the three most important points about why you like them.

Turning Notes to Text

Suppose you have been asked to write something about euthanasia (or mercy killing) in India. Your first task would be to research various articles, books, newspaper reports and the Internet to see what you can find.

Step 1

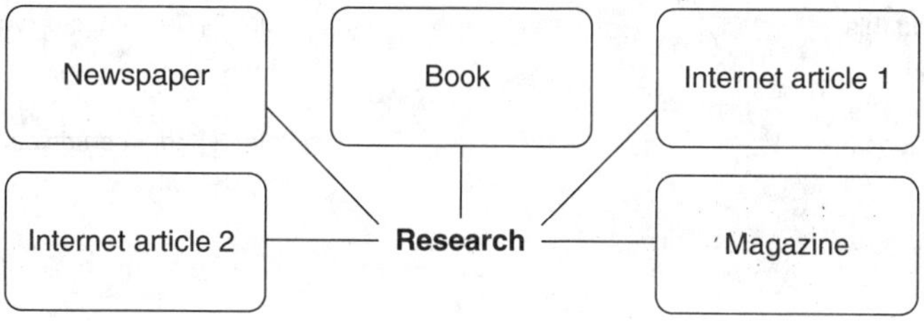

While doing your research, you need to make notes from each article. Ask the 'wh' questions mentioned earlier to write down the important points. Make two columns, one for the notes, and one for your comments on each point. Refer to the box on critical thinking in the group discussion chapter for help with writing down comments and asking questions. **Do not copy sentences from the articles.**

Step 2

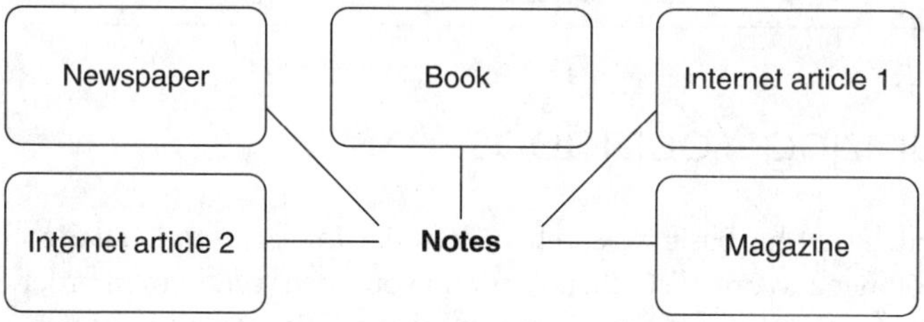

Then, you need to collate, that is, combine, all the notes and turn them into one set of notes and comments.

Step 3

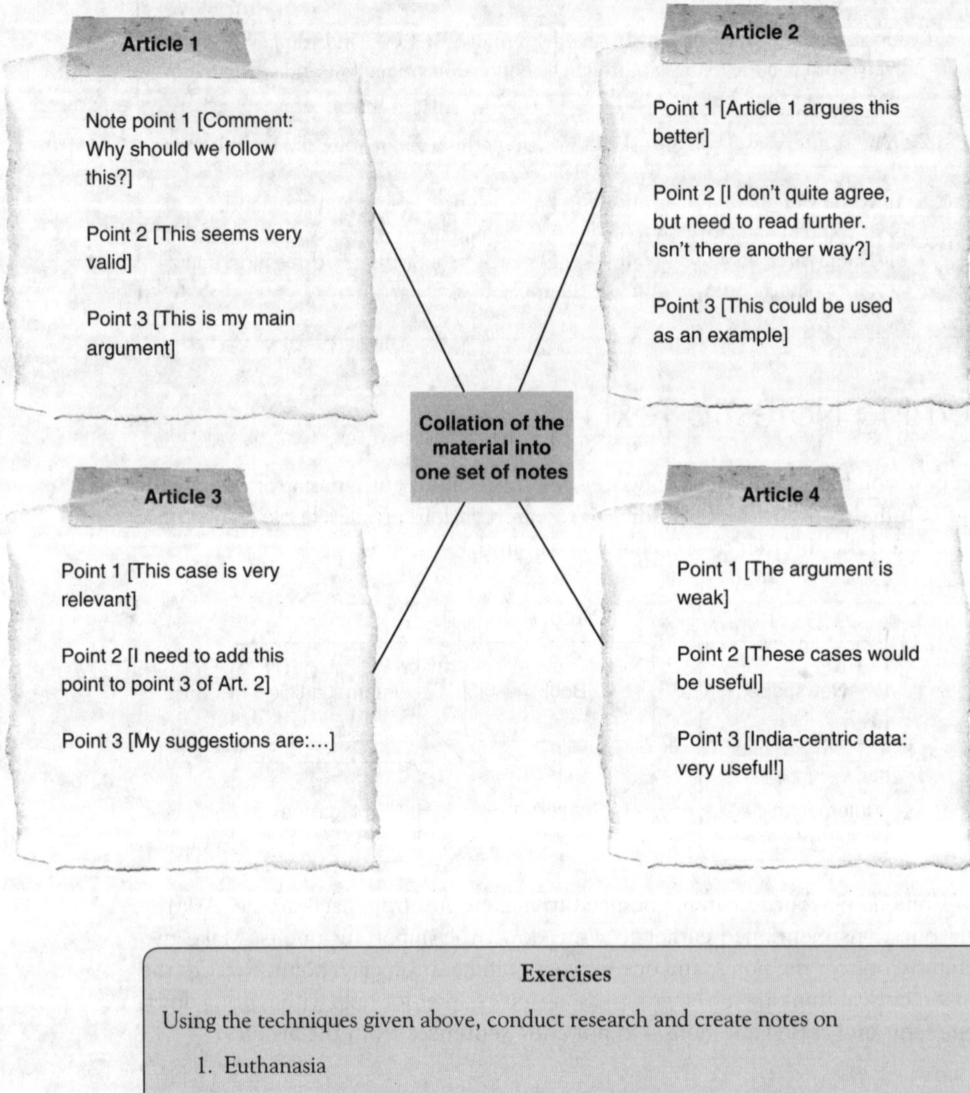

Exercises

Using the techniques given above, conduct research and create notes on

1. Euthanasia
2. Stem cell research

Organizing Your Ideas

Once you have the basic researched material in place and have collated your points, you need to organize the points and your ideas on them in order. There are several considerations you should have while organizing your material.

First, decide: (*a*) How long should be your essay? (*b*) Is it analytical [that is, you judge each point and comment on it], descriptive [you describe the

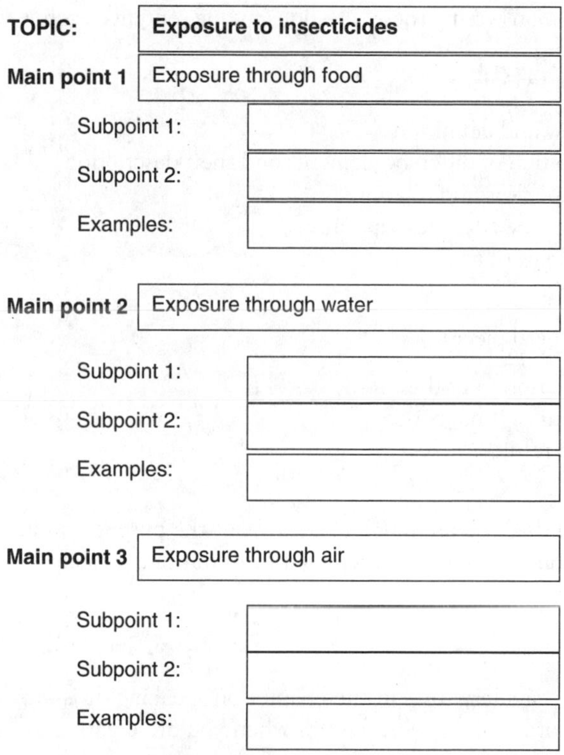

Figure A.4 Outlining

points one after another], or chronological [you describe events in time]? (c) Who is going to read it? These are three very important considerations. Once you've identified the kind of write-up you want to do, you need to organize your ideas in order of importance. Write down the main points without writing full sentences; write the key words that you would want to mention under each point. Specify all the examples you would want to add under each point (see Figure A.4).

You can also use the mind-mapping and Cornell note-taking techniques to organize your ideas. The main questions that you should ask when you are organizing your ideas are:

[For a critical piece]

1. For whom am I writing this piece?
2. What am I trying to say?
3. What are the major points I can state in my favour?
4. What kind of criticisms do I anticipate, and how can I answer them?
5. Is there any other kind of view that is possible, and why am I not considering it?

For any topic, try answering these questions in one sentence each.

[For a descriptive piece]

1. Overview and definition
2. Classification of different elements and their description
3. Their functions and relations
4. Drawings and their descriptions
5. Case studies (if any)
6. Conclusion

[For a chronological piece]

1. Brief description of the event
2. The event as it happened
3. The end result
4. Analyses

You will find that you are much clearer about the purpose, audience, and tone of your writing once you've organized your ideas in these formats.

Grouping

We discussed vocabulary trees in the chapter on speaking. It is important for you to create key word trees or word groups when you are creating outlines for your write-up from your notes. Let's say, for example, that you are writing an essay on a famous architect.

First, write down the key words you would use to describe him:

architect of modern India eminent engineer simple vegetarian teetotaller hardworking honest statesman visionary Bharat Ratna

Then, group the keywords into categories:

Personal	**Achievements**
simple	architect of modern India
vegetarian	eminent engineer
teetotaller	statesman
hardworking	visionary
honest	Bharat Ratna

This kind of grouping will help you develop a clear plan for writing the piece.

Cohesion and Coherence

Cohesion and coherence refer to the idea that what you say or write should come together as a logical piece; that is, one idea is connected to the next in meaning, each idea follows from another idea, and all the ideas together make up one clear point of view. Cohesion refers more specifically to connections between sentences, while coherence refers to the overall connectedness of ideas in a piece of writing. When audiences/readers ask the question, 'What was s/he trying to say?' the answer should be clear in their heads. Refer to what we said in the section on organizing your ideas. Once you have answered the questions given there, the write-up will be automatically much more logically *coherent*. We'll also discuss the question of coherence later, in the section on paragraph writing.

To make sentences *cohesive*, you need to ensure the following:

1. Have transition words that link sentences. This can be done by repeating some information from sentence A to sentence B. For example:

   By 2010, OPEC could easily produce half of the world's oil. This is because OPEC members control such a huge share of the world's high-quality, low-cost oil reserves.

2. Link the sentences thematically. Are all the sentences talking about the same thing, but advancing your ideas gradually? For example:

   A nuclear power reactor uses fission reactions to produce thermal energy that is converted to electrical energy.

   ↓

   One common class of nuclear reactor is the light water reactor which uses light water as a moderator and as a coolant.

   ↓

   There are two types of light water reactors: the pressurized water reactor and the boiling water reactor.

   All sentences talk about nuclear reactors, but every sentence gives new information.

3. Have parallel constructions: Sentences are also linked when one piece of information is compared or contrasted with another. For example:

   In ordinary speech, the word 'group' can mean any organization that involves more than two people. It can even mean crowds of people.

   ↑

   Contrasted with

   ↓

   In the social sciences, however, it refers to two or more people who have come together or belong together and are aware of their common connections. This awareness differentiates a crowd from a group.

Memos

In business communication, we often have to send day-to-day information to a specific set of people. Memos are the simplest form of written material. They are written like letters, but are different from letters in two aspects: they are not meant for one particular person and are therefore less private. Secondly, their format also tends to be less formal than that of a business letter. Figure A.5 shows the basic format of a simple memo.

TO: (readers' names and job titles)
FROM: (your name and job title)
DATE: (complete and current date)
SUBJ: (what the memo is about, highlighted in some way)

Please be informed that Mr XY from ABC Company will be visiting our office premises for a talk on optimal power usage on Tuesday, 2 August. He will be discussing the benefits of CFL use as well as those of using solar power. You are requested to assemble at the Longman Hall at 10 a.m. for a meeting with him.

If you have any questions for Mr XY, please submit them within 1 August in the suggestion box at the reception. He will be answering questions at the end of the session.

Figure A.5 Sample of a Short Memo

Internal Memorandum

TO: All employees
FROM: Kamal Agarwala, Human Resources
DATE: 15 June 2010
SUBJ: Parents' Mediclaim policy

Routes message efficiently, with all needed information

It has been a difficult task to get an insurance company to run a parents' policy for us under the current market conditions. However, because of the longstanding corporate relationship that we have with XYZ Company, they have agreed, provided we have at least 250 parents covered.

Enclosed is the premium calculation sheet and the disease-wise capping for the parents' mediclaim policy. Apart from the mentioned diseases in the list if you go for a hospitalization then you can use your sum insured amount.

We would once again like to reiterate that you will need to **bear the premium amount** for this policy and once you have joined the policy **you cannot withdraw** it in the following year and **there must be continued membership year on year**. Please note that once you have joined the policy you cannot withdraw in between and there is no mid year inclusion of the parents for the existing employees.

Presents the details of the policy

Sign and return the following no later than Friday, 20 June.

Yes, I am interested in the parents' policy and would like to pay Rs. ________ a month/quarter/half-yearly/annually.

No, I am not interested.

Signature:
Employee ID ____________

Provides an easy-to-use response form

Figure A.6 A Detailed Memo

Memos may also be detailed and provide important information about policies, etc. See, for example, Figure A.6.

Narrating Events Chronologically

Have you ever told stories to anyone? Narrative essays, or stories, usually follow a chronological order: first this happened, then this, then this. A narrative essay usually recreates an event for a purpose, that is, you obviously have something to say through a story.

Here's how a narrative essay should be organized: Introduction ⟶ First event ⟶ Second event ⟶ Third event ⟶ Ending (with main point).

Now, see the story given below. This is from the Aesop's fables collection.

The Lark and Her Young Ones

A lark had made her nest in the early spring on the young green wheat. The brood had almost grown to their full strength and attained the use of their wings and the full plumage of their feathers, when the owner of the field, looking over his ripe crop, said, 'The time has come when I must ask all my neighbours to help me with my harvest.' One of the young larks heard his speech and related it to his mother, asking her where they should move for safety. 'There is no occasion to move yet, my son,' she replied, 'the man who only sends to his friends to help him with his harvest is not really in earnest.' The owner of the field came again a few days later and saw the wheat shedding the grain from excess of ripeness. He said, 'I will come myself tomorrow with my labourers, and with as many reapers as I can hire, and will get in the harvest.' The lark, on hearing these words said to her brood, 'It is time now to be off, my little ones, for the man is in earnest this time; he no longer trusts his friends, but will reap the field himself.'

Moral of the story: Self-help is the best help.

Exercises

What we've given here is a very basic chronological essay. Now, write at least three paragraphs describing:

1. One of the most frightening experiences in your life.
2. A funny incident.
3. Your first day at school.
4. The lives of your grandparents.

Use the techniques given in the sections on paragraph writing for help.

Paragraph Writing

Have you ever been asked to write paragraphs on a topic? What does this mean? A paragraph is one of the central components of writing. The *Oxford Advanced Learners' Dictionary* defines it as 'a section of a piece of writing, usually consisting of several sentences dealing with a single subject'. A paragraph is 'a group of sentences or a single sentence that forms a unit'. Ultimately, good paragraphs contain a sentence or sentences unified around one central, controlling idea.

Imagine reading page after page of text without any paragraphs. It would be very difficult to read and comprehend. Therefore, when you are asked to write paragraphs, remember to *paragraph often*, so you don't scare your readers. Write short sentences, and write short paragraphs, each containing one main idea.

First line of the paragraph is indented from the left margin

A paragraph begins on a new line even if you have to leave most of the previous line empty. You may leave a line space before a paragraph begins, or you may 'indent' the first line of the paragraph.

In this book, we have used an indented style to mark each paragraph.

Parts of a Paragraph

Read the sections on note-taking and organizing again. Those sections will help you a lot to proceed from notes to writing paragraphs.

A paragraph is divided into three basic parts:

1. The topic sentence or main idea: This is the first sentence of the paragraph. It conveys the main idea of the paragraph to the readers and helps them focus on the theme as well as enables him/her to know what is going to be conveyed in it. You should summarize the main points of your paragraph in the first sentence.
2. Subpoints or supporting ideas: The rest of the paragraph consists of a series of sentences that develop, support or explain the main idea. They come after the topic sentence, forming the supporting details or the body of a paragraph. They give detailed information about the main idea through examples, illustrations, facts or stories. The information given in this part should be reliable, convincing and trustworthy.
3. The concluding sentence: The concluding or closing sentence is the last sentence of a paragraph. It sums up and restates the main idea as well as the details supported in the paragraph. It is the closing sentence that reminds readers what they should value. You should restate the main idea of the paragraph as well as summarize it using different words.

Writing a Good Paragraph

Writing a good paragraph or an essay involves some stages. You can use the acronym **TOWER** to recall the five steps involved in writing a paragraph or essay. **TOWER** stands for thinking, organizing, writing, editing and rewriting.

Thinking Focus on key words and phrases related to your topic. Think about how much information ought to be included for each topic.

Pre-writing stage

Organizing Organize information using techniques like outlining, flow charts, grouping and mind mapping.

Writing Write the first draft of the paragraph or essay.

Post-writing stage

Editing Look for mistakes in language and in the arrangement of your ideas.

Rewriting Correct all errors and write the final version.

The Pre-Writing Stage

Refer to the previous sections on thinking, making notes and organizing your ideas. We've given here a sample outline for paragraph writing.

Developing Outlines for Writing a Paragraph
Example: Reality Shows on TV

Success of reality shows ________ *a few successful shows* ________ *provide a platform to the budding talents, amuse us, enhance our knowledge* ________ *increase the burden* ________ *involve politics* ________ *game of power*

Reality shows are gaining a lot of popularity these days. In 1995, India's first TV show 'SA-REGA-MA' was shown on the national channel. As far as TRP (Television Rating Points) is concerned, it was a great success. The show not only had a large viewership but earned a lot of name and fame for its makers. Since then, the reality shows have become a usual practice to gain more and more popularity.

Many shows such as, *sa-re-ga-ma-pa, Close Up Antakshari, Meri Aawaz Suno, Indian Idol, Kaun Banega Crorepati?, Bigg Boss, Dus Ka Dum, Star Voice of India, Boogie Woogie* and many more have attained a huge popularity. Reality shows are planned according to the taste of the people. These shows are liked as they showcase the talent of the budding artists, provide the audience with healthy entertainment and guide the viewers in the right direction. Shreya Ghoshal, Kunal Ganjawala and Sunidhi Chauhan, the famous singers of the music industry have come from reality shows. Shilpa Shetty gained a lot of popularity as an international artist because of such a show named *Big Brother*. Some shows give us an opportunity to know the life of the film stars. While laughter shows contribute to the national health by relieving people of their day-to-day stress, the other shows like *KBC, Bournvita Quiz Contest* enhance our knowledge.

Dance and musical shows provide us with sheer amusement, keep us in touch with the latest trends and at the same time provide us an opportunity to give our judgement. Nevertheless, these shows have many shortcomings too. Such shows have increased burden on children. Not only do their studies suffer but also the pressure of competition gets accumulated them. Besides this, they take us away from our culture. To gain popularity, the show owners include gossip, controversies and fights. It is shown that the people win due to public opinion but it is, in fact, the game of power and money. To conclude, the reality shows are not always real.

Now, based on the above, develop outlines for the following topics: **Ragging; The Importance of Technical Education; Engineers: Builders of the Nation.**

The Writing Stage

This stage is when you turn your ideas into sentences.

Use language appropriate for your readers: As we stated earlier, the first question you ask when you begin to write paragraphs is 'Who is going to read this?'

Let us consider these two examples. The first one is from a report published in *Science*.[1]

> Mammalian histone lysine methyltransferase, suppressor of variegation 39H1 (SUV39H1), initiates silencing with selective methylation on Lys^9 of histone H3, thus creating a high-affinity binding site for HP1. When an antibody to endogenous SUV39H1 was used for immunoprecipitation, MeCP2 was effectively coimmunoprecipitated; conversely, αHA antibodies to HA-tagged MeCP2 could immunoprecipitate SUV39H1.

This kind of language would be extremely difficult for most students to understand, not to mention being very technical. This is best suited for highly specialized research articles. Now see this:

> When a heart attack occurs, the dying part of the heart may trigger electrical activity that causes *ventricular fibrillation*. This is an uncoordinated twitching of the ventricles that replaces the smooth, measured contractions that pump blood to the body's organs. Many times if trained medical professionals are immediately available, they can use electrical shock to start the heart beating again.
>
> If the heart can be kept beating and the heart muscle is not too damaged, small blood vessels may gradually reroute blood around blocked arteries. This is called *collateral circulation*.[2]

For the most part, this sample, though technical in theme, uses everyday words like *trigger*, *twitching* and *blocked*. The two technical words, *ventricular fibrillation* and *collateral circulation*, are well-defined.

No matter how technical the subject, try to use simple language so that your readers can understand what you're saying. Avoid using long words: say *use* instead of *utilize*; don't *initiate* and *terminate* things—*start* and *stop* them.

Use a reasonable sentence length: Long sentences are difficult to read and will bore your readers. Sentences that exceed 40 or 50 words are too difficult for most people to read. Professional writers try to keep the average sentence length at 20 words or so.

Organize your ideas in space and time: This is an important consideration, especially in the description of events or processes. Are you writing about an event? Remember to develop a clear time outline based on how something happened. What are the related stories you want to develop along each point?

Describing an Event	
What happened	Describe the events in brief and give an introduction to the paragraph, including what you plan to do.
When did it happen?	Develop a detailed timeline of what happened after what. Add subpoints next to each point for your comments.
Analysis	What is your overall opinion/stance? Summarize and critically review the points to come to a conclusion about the event. Suggest points for action if you wish to.
Describing a Process	
What are you describing?	Give an idea, in brief, of what you trying to describe. Provide definitions and examples.
Outlines for the process	Precisely identify every step in your outline, where one step follows from another. Every step should have the following elements: the definition of the process, how it happens, and its functions and uses. Accompany the steps with diagrams and figures, if necessary. Figures should be properly labelled.
Conclusion	Summarize all the points discussed.

Ensure coherence: As we discussed earlier, coherence means a logical relationship between the ideas and the presentation. For a paragraph to be coherent, the sentences should be arranged in a logical manner and should follow a definite plan for development. To achieve coherence in a paragraph, you need to use pronouns and linking words appropriately:

- Pronouns—*this/that/these/those*—should be used carefully to maintain continuity; otherwise, they will confuse readers.
- Sentence linkers such as *first/meanwhile/later /afterwards/finally/at that time/ at that very moment/next to/in front of/besides* can be used to join sentences in space and time.
- Sequence words like *between/behind/after/then/now* are used to show chronological order or sequence.
- Linking words—*thus/therefore/hence/ however/as a result of/accordingly/due to/ owing to/consequently/similarly/likewise/yet/nevertheless/on the other hand/on the contrary*, etc.—present the objects or situations in comparison or contrast to one another as well as explain them.
- Transition words—furthermore/*in fact/in addition to/for example/ as an illustration/ for instance/in other words*, etc.—help the writer describe ideas or objects.

- Conclusion words like *to conclude/to sum up/to summarize/in short/in a nutshell* conclude or summarize the piece and words such as *definitely/certainly/of course/no doubt/undoubtedly* restate or reaffirm the ideas.

Provide citations: If you have taken any material/quote, idea from other sources, do not forget to mention the details of the source. Taking material from other sources without acknowledgement is unethical and should be avoided at all costs. Towards the end of this chapter, we've provided a template of a formatted document. You will see that we have referred to three sources for the text and one each for the table and figure. The details of the text sources are given under the 'Notes' section.

We shall discuss citation and references in detail in Chapter 9.

The Post-Writing or Editing Stage

When you've written the first draft of the paragraphs using this chapter's guidelines, it is a good idea, especially if you are writing alone, to share it with a friend or, even better, one of your identified readers. Ask this person to read your draft, check it for accuracy and completeness, and suggest ideas for revision. Then revise it again, if necessary, taking in your reader's suggestions.

If you are writing with others, your team will need to combine your revised individual sections into a common document. It is very important to check such a document for consistency in language, style and overall coherence, since different people have different ways of writing.

Exercises

Use a sample of your own writing to see whether you can improve it using the guidelines described in this chapter. Identify paragraphs, sentences, or word choices that could be improved. Describe your writing and explain why the portions you have identified need revision, and then revise them.

You must, yourself, check the word choices, spellings, grammar, punctuation, handwriting and form. There should be no long, unwinding sentences, no repetitions, no complex examples or difficult terms. Instead of definitions, give examples and supporting details. No irrelevant information should be given. Read your paragraph again. Make sure each sentence has a subject. See if the **subjects and verbs agree** with each other. Check the verb tenses of each sentence. Make sure that each sentence makes sense, your paragraph has a topic sentence and your supporting sentences focus on the main idea. Ensure that you have a closing sentence. Finally, see if your paragraph is interesting.

Subject-Verb Agreement

The basic principle of subject–verb agreement is that *singular subjects need singular verbs; plural subjects need plural verbs*.

Important points to remember:

- The indefinite pronouns *anyone, everyone, someone, no one, nobody* are always singular and, therefore, require singular verbs. Everyone is, Someone has, Each of the students is, etc.
- The word 'some' may or may not take a plural verb, depending of what they are referring to: Some of the cards are, Some of the water is, etc.
- Phrases such as *together with, as well as,* and *along with* are not the same as *and*:

    The policeman as well as his brothers **is** going to prison.
    The policeman and his brothers **are** going to prison.

- Either and neither take singular verbs: Either of them is fine; Neither of them is okay.
- Or and nor take singular or plural verbs, depending on the subject closer to the verb:

    Either my sister or my brothers **are** going to the market.
    Neither my brothers nor my sister **is** going to the market.
    Are either my brothers or my sister going?
    Is either my sister or my brothers going?

Find out more about subject-verb agreement in order to be confident about your written English.

Editing and proofreading your draft: Refer to the section on organizing your ideas. We had given a sample of grouping key words to write a paragraph on an architect. Now, after going through the sections on pre-writing and writing, imagine that you have written a rough draft. See this draft given here.

Exercises

Editing a Draft Paragraph

Check and correct all spelling, grammar, punctuation and other errors that you can locate in the document. Rewrite it to make it better and add paragraph breaks wherever necessary. What words would you change and why? We've solved this one for you at the end of the chapter, but refer to it only after you have done the work yourself.

Sir Mokshagundam visvesvaraya was an eminent engineer and statesman who played a key role in building of modern India. He received our country highest honour, the Bharat Ratna in 1955. He was responsible for building the very first electricity generation plant in Asia at Shivanasamudram near Mysore in 1894. He had many acheivement to his credit these include implementing an extremely intricate system of irrigation in the Deccan area, designing and patenting a system of automatic weir water floodgates, and supervising the construction of the KRS dam across the Cauvery River from concept to inauguration. The automatic flood gates designed were first installed in 1903 at the Khadakvasla reservoir near Pune. These gates were employed to rise the flood supply level of storage in the reservoir to the highest level likely to be attained by its flood without causing any damage to the dam. Based on the success of these gates, the same system was installed at the Tigra dam in Gwalior and the Krishnaraja Sagara (KRS) dam in Mysore. Visvesvaraya achieved celebrity status when

> he designed a flood protection system to protect the city of Hyderabad floods. He was also instrumental in developing a system to protect Vishakapatnam port from sea erosion. Sir M. V. supervised the construction of the KRS dam across the Cauvery River from concept to inauguration. This dam created the biggest reservoir in Asia at the time it was built. During his period of service with the Government of Mysore state, he was responsible for founding of under the aegis of that government the Mysore Soap Factory, the Parasitoid laboratory, the Bhadravati Iron & Steel Works, the SJ Polytechnic Institute, the Bangalore Agricultural University, the State Bank of Mysore, the Mandya Sugar Mills and numerous other industrial ventures. He also encouraged private investment in industry during his tenure as Diwan of Mysore.

Once you've edited the draft and made all the changes, you need to go through the text again, that is, *proofread* the text, to see that all errors have been taken care of. Now your text material is ready to be styled and formatted.

Styling and formatting your text: Even if your text is well-written and edited, it will be difficult to read if the font size is too small or too large. If the write-up is long, then appropriate headings are necessary to break up the text thematically. Follow the basic guidelines of division from the outlines you initially created (Main idea, subpoints, examples, etc.). Add a heading to every main idea, and the paragraphs will be easier to read.

The standard format is to type your text in 12 pt, Times New Roman. Justify the text, provide paragraph breaks in the form of new lines or indents, provide a title to the document and headings for every main idea. The text will be easier to read if you double-space it. Set wide margins so that the text doesn't look very heavy on the eye.

The title should be centre-aligned, in a larger and/or different size, and the headings should also stand out. Let's review the sample document here. Note all the elements that have been formatted. If you have figures, tables, and other elements, they need to be typed in a different font size/type.

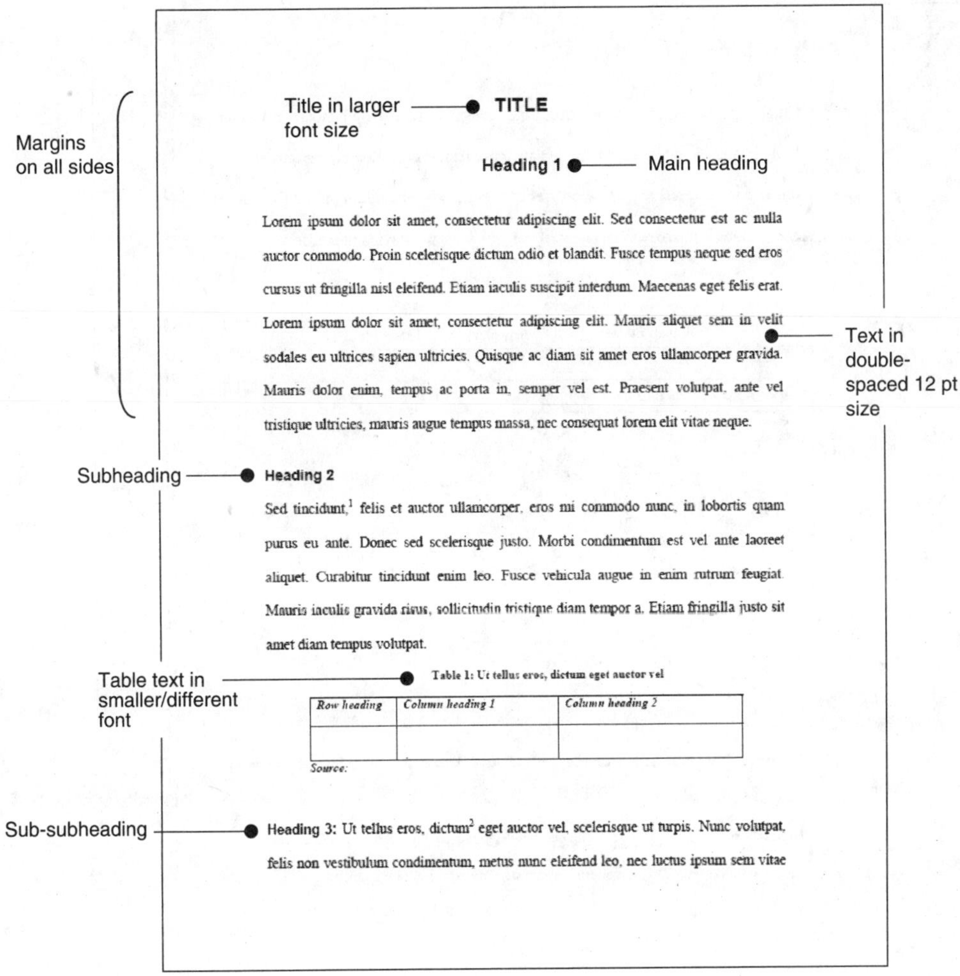
Title in larger font size
TITLE
Margins on all sides
Heading 1
Main heading
Lorem ipsum dolor sit amet, consectetur adipiscing elit. Sed consectetur est ac nulla auctor commodo. Proin scelerisque dictum odio et blandit. Fusce tempus neque sed eros cursus ut fringilla nisl eleifend. Etiam iaculis suscipit interdum. Maecenas eget felis erat. Lorem ipsum dolor sit amet, consectetur adipiscing elit. Mauris aliquet sem in velit sodales eu ultrices sapien ultricies. Quisque ac diam sit amet eros ullamcorper gravida. Mauris dolor enim, tempus ac porta in, semper vel est. Praesent volutpat, ante vel tristique ultricies, mauris augue tempus massa, nec consequat lorem elit vitae neque.
Text in double-spaced 12 pt size
Subheading
Heading 2
Sed tincidunt,1 felis et auctor ullamcorper, eros mi commodo nunc, in lobortis quam purus eu ante. Donec sed scelerisque justo. Morbi condimentum est vel ante laoreet aliquet. Curabitur tincidunt enim leo. Fusce vehicula augue in enim rutrum feugiat. Mauris iaculis gravida risus, sollicitudin tristique diam tempor a. Etiam fringilla justo sit amet diam tempus volutpat.
Table text in smaller/different font
Table 1: Ut tellus eros, dictum eget auctor vel
Row heading
Column heading 1
Column heading 2
Source:
Sub-subheading
Heading 3: Ut tellus eros, dictum2 eget auctor vel, scelerisque ut turpis. Nunc volutpat, felis non vestibulum condimentum, metus nunc eleifend leo, nec luctus ipsum sem vitae

neque. Curabitur vitae enim eros, at varius ante. Integer lacus eros, bibendum at lacinia et, rutrum ac quam. Ut in lobortis nulla. Sed auctor nulla nec odio elementum quis aliquet ante tristique. Morbi at nisl augue. Donec vel urna et mauris fermentum ornare rhoncus a arcu. Aenean id nunc in ante mollis faucibus. Vivamus ornare gravida dapibus.[3]

Source citation

Figure 1: Ut tellus eros, dictum eget auctor vel

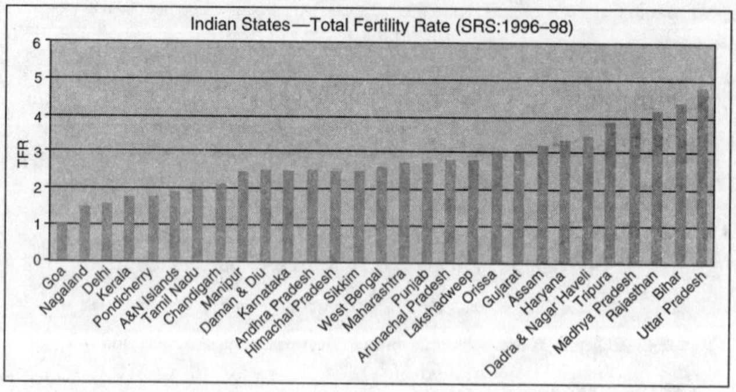

Source:

Notes

1. Curabitur vitae enim eros, at varius ante. Integer lacus eros, bibendum at lacinia et, rutrum ac quam.
2. Ut in lobortis nulla. Sed auctor nulla nec odio elementum quis aliquet ante tristique.
3. Morbi at nisl augue. Donec vel urna et mauris fermentum ornare rhoncus a arcu. Aenean id nunc in ante mollis faucibus. Vivamus ornare gravida dapibus.

Details of sources and other comments

Edited Draft

Sir Mokshagundam Visvesvaraya was an eminent engineer and statesman who played a key role in building modern India. He received our country's highest honour, the Bharat Ratna, in 1955. He had many achievements to his credit. These include implementing an extremely intricate system of irrigation in the Deccan area, designing and patenting a system of automatic weir water floodgates, and supervising the construction of the KRS dam across the Cauvery river from concept to inauguration. The automatic floodgates were first installed in 1903 at the Khadakvasla reservoir near Pune. These gates were used to raise the flood supply level of storage in the reservoir to the highest level likely to be attained by a flood, without causing any damage to the dam. Based on the success of these gates, the same system was installed at the Tigra dam in Gwalior and the Krishnaraja Sagara (KRS) dam in Mysore. Sir Mokshagundam was also responsible for building the very first electricity generation plant in Asia at Shivanasamudram near Mysore, as early as 1894.

Sir Mokshagundam achieved celebrity status when he designed a flood protection system to protect the city of Hyderabad from floods. He was also instrumental in developing a system to protect Vishakapatnam port from sea erosion. The KRS dam was the biggest reservoir in Asia at the time it was built.

During his service with the Government of Mysore, Sir Mokshagundam was responsible for founding, under the aegis of that government, the Mysore Soap Factory, the Parasitoid Laboratory, the Bhadravati Iron & Steel Works, the SJ Polytechnic Institute, the Bangalore Agricultural University, the State Bank of Mysore, the Mandya Sugar Mills and numerous other industrial ventures. He also encouraged private investment in industry during his tenure as Diwan of Mysore.

Deleted: visvesvaraya

Deleted: of

Deleted: He was responsible for building the very first electricity generation plant in Asia at Shivanasamudram near Mysore in 1894.

Deleted: these

Deleted: River

Deleted:

Deleted: designed

Deleted: employed

Deleted: its

Formatted: Indent: First line: 0.5"

Deleted: Visvesvaraya

Deleted: Sir M. V. supervised the construction of the KRS dam across the Cauvery River from concept to inauguration.

Deleted: is

Deleted: created

Deleted: during

Deleted: period of

Deleted: state

Deleted: he

Deleted: of

Deleted: laboratory

Sir Mokshagundam Visvesvaraya was an eminent engineer and statesman who played a key role in building modern India. He received our country's highest honour, the Bharat Ratna, in 1955. He had many achievements to his credit. These include implementing an extremely intricate system of irrigation in the Deccan area, designing and patenting a system of automatic weir water floodgates, and supervising the construction of the KRS dam across the Cauvery river from concept to inauguration. The automatic floodgates were first installed in 1903 at the Khadakvasla reservoir near Pune. These gates were used to raise the flood supply level of storage in the reservoir to the highest level likely to be attained by a flood, without causing any damage to the dam. Based on the success of these gates, the same system was installed at the Tigra dam in Gwalior and the Krishnaraja Sagara (KRS) dam in Mysore. Sir Mokshagundam was also responsible for building the very first electricity generation plant in Asia at Shivanasamudram near Mysore, as early as 1894.

Sir Mokshagundam achieved celebrity status when he designed a flood protection system to protect the city of Hyderabad from floods. He was also instrumental in developing a system to protect Vishakapatnam port from sea erosion. The KRS dam was the biggest reservoir in Asia at the time it was built.

During his service with the Government of Mysore, Sir Mokshagundam was responsible for founding, under the aegis of that government, the Mysore Soap Factory, the Parasitoid Laboratory, the Bhadravati Iron & Steel Works, the SJ Polytechnic Institute, the Bangalore Agricultural University, the State Bank of Mysore, the Mandya Sugar Mills and numerous other industrial ventures. He also encouraged private investment in industry during his tenure as Diwan of Mysore.

Notes

1. Quoted from Victoria V. Lunyak, et al., 'Corepressor-Dependent Silencing of Chromosomal Regions Encoding Neuronal Genes', *Science*, 2002, Vol. 298. no. 5599, pp. 1747–52, p. 1748.
2. Text of the American Heart Association, http://www.healthscout.com/ency/68/243/main.html, accessed on 2 August 2010.

Appendix 3: Report Writing

Introduction

Report writing is a typical form of writing, different from expressive expository or descriptive writing. Report writing requires give and take, a dialogue, a follow-up, input and action. Most often, it creates action; it causes the person at the other end to react or respond. It is also a form of documentation where processes are described, recorded and analysed.

There are three factors determining report writing: purpose, audience and tone. The purpose of writing and the audience very often set the tone of a piece of writing. If you are writing a report solely for the purpose of documenting, your language will be different. But if you are presenting a proposal and trying to convince your colleagues, your tone will have to be persuasive.

Report writing is very specifically aimed at achieving certain purposes. A good training manual will do exactly what it is intended to do. Similarly, a well written marketing report or a feasibility report has very specific goals to achieve and they are tailored to fulfill those specific purposes only. A well designed and well-written piece of report writing has to take into consideration some important factors even before the process of writing begins.

Defining the Objectives

A well-written report has to define the objectives very specifically at the outset. The writer has to be very clear about:

1. Why the document is being written. Is it being written to simply record a process and keep it for reference or is it a proposal or plan which one wants

others to accept or is one trying to convince somebody that the proposed plan of action is undesirable or desirable.

2. What exactly is the writing intended to do?

Reports are generally written to convey information. It can be aimed at giving the reader information he/she desired to have or it can be aimed at changing the readers' response or attitude towards an object, a proposal or process. Or it can aim at giving the reader a set of instructions for the nursing procedure. To do this, the writer has to have a clear idea of the subject. Identifying the information the readers want the communication to provide. Determining how the audience will look for this information. This can be done by presenting the material in the form of:

- Points and Sub-points: Presenting the relevant facts as easily accessible points and sub-points.
- Tables: Putting the facts you want your readers to compare and contrast in the form of a table.
- Flow Charts: If you want your audience to quickly compare the lengths of two processes you could present both in the form of two flow charts on the same page. This will make comparison and assessment easy for the readers.

Identifying and Assessing the Audience

The most important point one has to take into account while preparing a report is the audience. Unlike other writings, report has a very specific audience. It is always important thus to identify the audience and prepare the document accordingly. If the document is meant for a medically literate audience, it can make prolific use of technical terms. This can make the document precise and compact, giving extra information only where necessary. If the audience is non-medical, however, the document has to be accordingly designed. The amount of information to be given depends on what the document will be used for. If the document is meant to educate the audience on a nursing procedure, it should be carefully designed keeping in mind the expected audience. If it is meant to issue instructions for a nursing procedure, on the other hand, it has to be presented in the form of a list of instructions or a flow chart.

Organization and Language

After deciding why the document is to be written, the objectives it is supposed to fulfil and the audience it is meant for, the most important factors you must concentrate on are the organization and the language.

To write with clarity one has to first have an outline of what one is going to present. There is no specific format for an outline; it has to be variable and flexible to suit the subject and scope of coverage. To have a good outline you must have:

- A clear emphatic summary of the subject matter.
- The perspective from which you are looking at it.
- Evidence in support of the thesis.

Some of the other elements that can be used to make writing more organized are:

- Introduction to the subject matter.
- Headings in large fonts to express transition to new ideas.
- Bulleted lists to draw attention to the subject matter and to make, comprehension easy.
- Use of figures, illustration, diagrams and graphs to give visual representation of what is being said.
- A summary that restates the main idea and emphasizes the perspective.

Synopsis Writing

Before you understand abstract writing, it is important to know the skill of summarizing. Summarizing is a highly functional skill as it is used by different kinds of learners and professionals to present a gist of what they have heard or read. A summary can be of a passage, a letter, a speech, a chapter or a book. The act of summarizing consists of separating the relevant points from the irrelevant ones, arranging the ideas systematically in a logical sequence, condensing the material in as short a form as possible. A summary may be half or quarter or a tenth of the original passage. While summarizing, you have to avoid using the same words, phrases and expressions used in the text. You have to rephrase the material in simple language. Comments, abbreviations, symbols and examples are avoided while summarizing. However, an abstract is a brief summary of the contents of a research report, article or presentation. When an abstract stands alone, separate from a paper or poster, the title and author(s) are added to give it context. Traditionally, the abstract covers an Introduction, Methods, Results and Discussion (IMRaD format) in the shortest amount of space possible.

> ***Title:*** This is the most succinct statement of your work. If you could define your research in one catchy, concise, concrete statement, this would be it.
> ***Authors:*** List authors and institutional affiliations according to the preferred method in your field. For instance, in computational sciences, the standard is to list authors alphabetically. The presenting author (you) will be distinguished from your co-authors on the submission form. Affiliations must follow each authors name unless the authors are from the same institution.
> ***Abstract (Body):*** There are four key elements in the body of an abstract:
>
> 1. Introduction: Problem Description, Motivation and Relevance
> 2. Methods
> 3. Results
> 4. Discussion (or Conclusions)

These four key elements comprise the IMRaD organizational format.

Exercises

Abridge the following sentences.

a. He refused to accept the explanation given by the nurse.
b. I cannot do this unless I have the instruments, which are necessary for the work.
c. After a thorough investigation was made, it was decided to make an exact estimate of the value of the property that was damaged.
d. The immediate objectives or the short-term goals of any organization are present along with the necessity of having long-term goals or goals of longer range. Even while the incessant fight with daily crises like supervising, hiring, selling and profit making goes on, any forward-looking organization is also concerned with the company's general growth, reputation and more importantly, creating and establishing an identity.
e. An appropriate understanding of a plan by the people who are concerned with a company plays an essential part in its fulfillment. They should all be able to understand the main lines or the direction in which development is expected to proceed in the future. They should also be able to see the progress in different directions and establish the links necessary to relate to one another and see how it can be strengthened and how firmly establishing one area can help in strengthening other areas too.

Report

Reports are among the most common types of communication used during work. Reports can be of various kinds. For instance it can be a 200-page report based on the research activities in genetic engineering to make improved food crops. It can be a 12-page report on the medical history of a patient. It can also be a 50-page report on a new kind of alarm system that has been devised to prevent car theft.

Formats for Report Writing

Reports vary in style, subject matter and presentation. Reports can be classified on various parameters, such as:

- Presentation—oral and written reports
- Length—short and long reports
- Nature—informal and formal reports
- Purpose—informational and analytical reports
- Time Duration—routine/periodic and special reports

1. **Oral Reports:** An oral report is a face-to-face communication about something seen, observed, experienced or investigated. It generally consists of impressions, observations and experiences. It is simple and easy to describe, quick and immediate to present and gives first-hand information but it may not be as objective and as detailed as a report has to be. It saves time for the reporter but may be strenuous for the listener as he/she has

to listen and memorize each and every word at the moment. Moreover, it lacks authenticity and is difficult to preserve. An oral report may not be used for taking vital decisions but it is beneficial in judging speculations and impressions and can be used to take an immediate action.

2. **Written Reports:** A written report provides a permanent record; so, it is always preferred to an oral report. Moreover, a written report is accurate and precise while an oral report may be vague at times. There are no chances of distortion of facts while transferring information from one source to another. A written report is more formal than an oral report and is generally used to communicate complex facts. It is a visual aid to communication as the reporter may organize message into paragraphs highlighting the main points.
3. **Short Reports:** Short reports can be presented in the form of a letter or a memo. They are concerned primarily with day-to-day business problems as well as their solutions. A short report consists of three parts—an opening, body and ending. Short reports, generally include periodic, situational and progress reports.
4. **Long Reports:** Long reports describe a problem in detail. They include the process of preparing the outline of the topic, collecting data, making a rough draft, logical and organized presentation of facts, thorough revising, editing and preparing the fair draft, etc. These reports require a deep study of an issue. The important parts of a long report are—preface, introduction, summary, abstract, description, conclusion, appendices, glossary and index.
5. **Informal Reports:** Certain business reports can be short and informal. In current business dealings, informal reports are more frequent than the formal ones. Basically, informal reports perform the same function as the formal reports—transmitting information, facts or data to someone for taking decision. However, informal reports are quite brief (around one to five pages), that too when you have supplementary material such as bibliography, appendices, etc. The style of writing is positive, personal and conversational. Depending on the requirement, they may have heading, illustrations, footnotes, etc., but may not include all the details like formal reports. Informal reports are written in the form of memo reports or letter reports.
6. **Formal Reports:** A formal report is the result of thorough investigation of a problem or situation. Formal reports are generally detailed and elaborate. These reports follow a fixed format. The length of the report may vary according to the requirement. Formal reports include informational, analytical, routine, special, technical, project, research reports, etc.
7. **Informational Reports:** An informational report presents facts, situations or problems required to take vital decisions. The writer collects relevant information, compiles and organizes it in an orderly manner and presents it as objectively as possible. Informational reports record happenings such as conferences, seminars, tours, and so on and supply details for future planning.
8. **Analytical Reports:** Analytical reports present data along with an analysis of it. The writer studies facts, situations or problems neutrally, evaluates the information, draws suitable inferences and puts forward his/her

recommendations and conclusions. Project reports, feasibility reports and market search reports fall in this category.

9. **Routine/Periodic Reports:** Routine reports, also known as form reports, are usually written on a prescribed proforma. The main purpose of these reports is to record the progress of a task, evaluate the performance of its employees and to record the success or failure of a policy. As these reports are written periodically, they are also called periodic reports. They generally include laboratory reports, progress reports, inspection reports, production reports, monthly sales reports, annual confidential reports, etc. All the organizations, institutions, companies and research establishments depend on routine reports for various decisions.
10. **Special Reports:** Special reports are written to convey special information related to a single condition, situation, occasion or problem. These reports do not contain repeated information as they are written about the specific situations. Like other reports, these reports also help in decision making as some of the most important decisions are taken on the basis of special reports. Special reports include inquiry reports, research reports, thesis, dissertations, etc.

Progress Report

A progress report informs the readers about the progress and status of a long-term project. The project may be about installation of a factory, construction of a bridge or a residential colony or some research work carried out in an organization. These reports are written at the various stages of the project. The essential details included in these reports are title of the project, total work to be done, time allotted, date, work already done, work to be done, time required, future plans, remarks, name, signature and designation of the reporter.

Incident Report

Incident repots document the exact details of the occurrence while they are fresh in the minds of those who witnessed the event. This information may be useful in the future when dealing with liability issues stemming from the incident.

A good incident report covers six important questions: Who? What? Where? When? Why? and How?

Consider a workplace situation that requires intervention by the management in order to resolve conflict. The people involved are separately asked to report the incident in writing. Some of them incorrectly document information they were witness to or were a part of. Consequently, the management refuses to acknowledge or act on the charges claim because the reports were conflicting. The victim fails to bring attention to the misdeeds of his colleague. Fighting to get the actual fats communicated will be a nightmare, because the information failed to be clear, accurate or specific in a report.

Well-written reports require some effort. They should not be something you merely throw together between calls. You should carefully review and edit each report before filing it or forwarding it to your supervisor. Consider reviewing the report with your crew before submitting it. Make sure it accurately reflects what each member did.

Remember!

- An incident report is factually accurate and objective
- It is complete, clear and concise in all respects
- An incident report does not confuse someone who wasn't there
- Complete details of *who, what, when, where, why* and *how* are always provided
- It is well-organized and grammatically correct with proper punctuation and spelling
- It is light on abbreviations and avoids using terms/abbreviations/acronyms that readers may not be familiar with

Feasibility Report

A feasibility report is generally written as an evaluation of whether or not a particular course of action is desirable. It is written to help the decision makers choose between two or more courses of action. Sometimes the choice is between maintaining the status quo and choosing the alternative being suggested. Sometimes, the choice can even be between two or more choices when the decision about the change has already been taken. An automobile industry, for example, might be considering the possibility of using hard plastic for certain parts for which metal has always been used. The choice here could also be between hard-plastic or some other alloy recently discovered that is costly but more durable.

The feasibility report has to deal with all the possible choices. It has to make a very careful consideration of:

- The various alternatives or the alternative suggested.
- The methods used to test the viability of using the alternatives.
- The advantages and disadvantages of the various alternatives. (This can be presented in a tabular form to make comparison at a single glance.)
- The alternative that you think is viable and why.

Structure of feasibility report

The introduction of the feasibility report is generally the answer to the question: Why should we consider these alternatives? For this, one has to do the following:

- Identify the problem the feasibility report will help solve; whether this will solve the existing problem, result in increased productivity or reduce the number of rejected parts.
- The introduction should also study the alternative courses of action you have considered. This will give the reader a broader scope of alternatives to think about before deciding on any one particular option.
- The introduction should contain the methods used to investigate and arrive at the conclusions.
- The introduction of long feasibility reports could also contain the preview of the main points in the conclusion and also the recommendations.

Remember!

- A feasibility report is written to help people choose between alternatives. Present the alternatives carefully.
- State the methods you have used for investigation.
- Decide how to present the matter for evaluation after carefully considering what the reader needs from the report.
- Always put the most important point first.
- Mention your conclusion more than once, with the Summary, the Introduction (if necessary) and in the Conclusion.
- Make firm and sensible recommendations. After all, you've studied the problem minutely.

Marketing Report

These reports contain guidelines for the promoters of the new products, policies, organizations, etc. Market research is an organized effort to gather information about markets or customers. It is done for discovering what people want, need, or believe or how they act. Once that research is completed, it can be used to determine how to market the product. This report collects data on market trends, users and prices of different commodities.

Format of a Marketing Report

1. Profile of the firm on which the study is being conducted
2. Introduction to the research work
3. Objectives of the research work (both Primary and Secondary)
4. Scope of the research work
5. Limitations of the research work
6. Research Methodology
7. Research Design
    - Sample Size
    - Sampling Method
    - Primary Data
    - Secondary Data
    - Methods of data collation
    - Methods of data analysis
8. Fact sheets in graphical, pie chart or diagram firm to present the number of users using a particular brand and its detailed interpretation
9. Fact sheets in graphical, pie chart or diagram firm to present the factors influencing the purchasing inclination of the clients and its detailed interpretation
10. Fact sheets in graphical, pie chart or diagram firm to present the satisfaction level of the clients and its detailed interpretation
11. References
12. Conclusion

Field Report

Formal report compiled and communicated by field engineers or other onsite personnel for off-site personnel. We all observe people, interactions and events in everyday life; however, your job when writing a field report is more structured. When writing a field report you need to:

- Systematically observe and accurately record in detail the varying aspects of a situation
- Constantly analyse your observation for meaning (i.e., what's going on here? what does this mean? what else does this relate to?)
- Keep the report's aims in mind while you are observing
- Consciously observe, record and analyse what you hear and see in the context of a theoretical framework/s

Field reports need not have a specific format, as the requirements change according to the situation of creating the report. However it should have these essential elements:

- Description – what you have seen or observed
- Analysis – strengths and weaknesses, reflection or evaluation of observations in light of theory and key concepts of your course or the broader context of your discipline
- Appendix – information that supports your analysis but is not essential to its explanation i.e. full transcripts of observation, maps, court session details

Laboratory Test Report

A laboratory report records the experimental work done in a laboratory to analyze a theory, conclusion or validity of a particular research. One has to record the process, reactions and results accurately to arrive at a convincing conclusion. These reports include title, experiment number, date, purpose, apparatus used, procedure adopted, observations, conclusions and signature.

Format of a laboratory test report

Title Page

The title should be concise and refer to the major variables or theoretical issues under investigation. *The title should be explanatory when standing alone.* Do not use abbreviations, and avoid phrases like 'Experimental Investigation of…', 'A discussion on the basis of…', or 'A Study of…'.

Abstract

This is your one-paragraph summary of the research/experiment conducted. The abstract should be about 100–150 words. This will be a brief description of the issue under investigation, the participants, the experiments conducted, the method used, the results and the conclusions drawn from the findings.

(Continued)

Introduction

An introduction must address two questions:

1. What has been done in the particular field by other researchers till date?
2. What is the objective of the present study?

This section will document the history of research in the field. You might describe the inconsistency in prior findings in this field of research. Proceed to explain how your experiment may simplify the problem and solve it. Explain your research findings on the basis of which you will state your hypothesis. This should be done at the end of the introduction, after you have explained the research and thinking that led to it. Identify independent and dependent variables here. You may want to include a sentence or two about the operations that you have adhered to. If you have made predictions about the outcome of the study, say so. Be clear and confident about the results that you expect. The readers will not guess what you are thinking. In the introduction, you are moving from the general to the specific: a general discussion of the problem area, to your specific hypothesis.

Method

In this section you will explain in detail the entire process of the experiment/research. This will include information on the participants, the materials/apparatus used, the procedures followed, and if required, a design/outline of the experiment/research. It is important to note here, that this section is meant to function as the guide to the experiment/research so that anyone else can conduct the entire process using the information supplied here. The following subsections must be included under Method.

Participants: The age, sex, and any other relevant demographic data are presented here. State how many subjects participated, how they were selected, and how they were assigned to groups.

Materials/Apparatus: A description of the apparatus used is given here. In the case of standard laboratory equipment, rather than describing the entire apparatus, the company name and model and/or serial number is sufficient. If this is not possible, the equipment should be described in detail. If materials (such as a questionnaire) were used, either cite your source (if published materials were used) or provide a copy in the appendix of your paper if you devised the instrument yourself.

Procedure: This will be a detailed description of the events that you (the experimenter) went through from the beginning until the end of the study. Experimental and control group assignment to conditions, order or manner of experimental treatment presentation and a summary of the instructions to the participants are presented here. You might also include a statement about your research design and the operational definitions of your variables.

(*Continued*)

Findings/Results: This section is where you present your data and analyses. The experimenter gives a description and not an explanation of the findings of the experiment. In order to fulfil this requirement, this section should include descriptive statistics (rather than the raw data) and statistical tests if used. Include degrees of freedom used, obtained values of inferential statistics performed, probability level, and direction of effect. Make reference to any figures and tables used, for example, '(see Table 9.1)', or 'as shown in Table 9.1. The reference to the table or figure should be close to the relevant material in the text. Never use a figure or table without referring to it in the text. Tables are often used when presenting descriptive statistics. Pictures, graphs, and drawings are referred to as figures. You should use as few tables and figures as possible. They should be used as supplements, not to do the entire job of communication.

Discussion/Stating the hypothesis: State your conclusions on the basis of your analyses. The conclusions should be related to the questions raised in your introduction section. How is this study, and these results, relevant to the field? You should open the discussion section with a statement of support or non-support for your original hypothesis. You may want to point out differences or similarities between other points of view (as stated in the Introduction) and your own. You may remark on certain shortcomings of the study, but avoid dwelling on flaws. In general, this section allows you to examine, interpret and qualify your results.

Project Report

Project reports usually provide pre-investment information required for investments before setting up the project. These reports are based on small investigations. Cost, goods, machinery requirements, etc., given in the report are rough calculations. They also keep the organizations regularly updated about the progress of the long-term projects or bring an important issue in the limelight.

The sequence in which the project report material should be arranged and bound should be as follows:

1. Cover Page and Title Page
2. Bonafide Certificate
3. Abstract
4. Table of Contents
5. List of Tables
6. List of Figures
7. List of Symbols, Abbreviations and Nomenclature
8. Chapters
9. Appendices
10. References

The table and figures shall be introduced in the appropriate places.

Leaflets and Brochures

Leaflets are printed sheets of either A4, A5, A6 size paper. The reason they are small is so that they can be easily handed out and kept. As leaflets are often only looked at fleetingly, the facts should be kept to a minimum. A brochure (also referred to as a pamphlet) is a type of leaflet. The two most common brochure styles are single sheet, and booklet (folded leaflets) forms.

Some key requirements to create an effective leaflet are:

- Grab the reader's attention
- Give a clear idea of what the reader is expected to do
- Keep that idea in the reader's mind, and
- Persuade the reader to take action

Consider the leaflet below with these elements in mind:

LOOKING FOR A QUIET GETAWAY FROM YOUR HECTIC CITY LIFE?

Then Kaddukhal will be perfect for you. Come, visit this tiny yet picturesque little town nestled in the lap of the Himalayas.

PLAY
Trekking, Camping and Mountaineering

A range of fun activities await the adventurous. Take part in them without worrying about your safety, since ample precautions have been taken on our part to make these activities absolutely free of any dangers.

EAT
Simple yet Delicious Kumauni Food

Bite into some delectable local dishes like Badi and Phanu made of lentils, rice and vegetables. Non-vegetarian food is also commonly available.

PRAY
The Temple of Sirkhanda Devi

Gain spiritual contentment by going on a short pilgrimage to the temple of the goddess, placed on top of an 8,000 foot high summit.

LIVE
Natural Beauty of the Hills

Be it the rich green foliage bordering every street or the beauty of the mountains on a moonlit night, the natural beauty of Kaddukhal will touch your heart and rejuvenate your soul.

(*Continued*)

Travel Details
Location: 30 miles from Mussoorie
Transport: Buses and taxis available
For more detail visit: www.travelkaddukhal.uttaranchal.com

We promise you an unforgettable experience.

Résumé

Résumé is a French word that means 'summary'. Although in English it is used to refer to 'an account or a summary of something', its popular use is limited to mean 'a brief account of an applicant's details to procure a job.' 'Résumé', pronounced as '*razume*', should not be confused with the word 'resume', uttered as '*rizum*', which distinctly means 'to begin again'. Professionally, a résumé is a document that contains a summary of the personal details, relevant job experience, education, skills, goals, achievements and interests of an applicant. It is the first item that an employer encounters regarding the job seeker to short list him/her for a job interview. Therefore, the primary aim of a résumé is to get a call for an interview, although securing the job is the ultimate objective.

CV

A CV is an abbreviation of 'curriculum vitae', which is defined as a written record of your education and experience that you send while applying for a job. Superficially, a CV and a résumé appear to be similar and may be considered comparable in some places but there are certain basic differences in their purposes, layouts and approaches:

1. CV is a traditional method of presenting personal data, while résumé evolved much later.
2. A résumé is normally used for seeking employment in business, finance and HR fields, especially in the private sector, whereas a CV is helpful while applying for academic, scientific, research, medical, university, fellowship and other educational positions.
3. A résumé is brief and concise—not more than a page or two. A CV is a longer version, a more detailed synopsis, extending up to four to five pages, perhaps more, in case annexure is attached.
4. By and large, a résumé has a free style and customarily enumerates a candidate's data in reverse chronological order, while a CV conveys chronologically arranged information.
5. A résumé highlights only the relevant credentials, while a CV provides a comprehensive summary of an applicant's personal, educational and career details.

In the United States, résumé is common in the business field while CV is used for academic positions. In some Asian countries such as India, the terms 'résumé' and 'CV' may be used interchangeably. Although, the use of résumé is fast gaining acceptance in the private business sector, some employers, especially government departments, may expect to receive a CV rather a résumé. Résumés are always position specific and they cannot be identical for different posts. The best way would be to prepare a standard CV, update it regularly and use it to design different versions of résumés as and when required.

Remember!

- A good résumé is designed for a specific post, arouses interest in the reader.
- It is well displayed with proper formatting, spacing and sufficient white space.
- It is factual, correct and complete.
- It provides information by categorizing under headings and columns.
- It uses appropriate concise style rather than using 'I' repeatedly.
- It is coherent, uniform and brief in presentation (preferably not more than one to two pages).
- It does not make overstated assertions.
- It highlights relevant areas starting from the recent ones.
- It uses right words, grammar, spelling and punctuation.

Styles of résumé

Résumés may be organized in two styles:

(a) Reverse chronological résumé: This is the most commonly used format. It gives the data in a reverse chronological order, as the employers today are more interested in your recent achievements. Such résumés go well for both a fresher and a beginner.

(b) Functional résumé: This is basically a skill profile that is used to focus on abilities that are specific to the type of position sought for. These résumés present details skill wise. They are suitable for those who want to change their career, have a wide work experience or are applying for jobs that require clearly defined profile and personality traits.

Components of a résumé/CV

We have seen that a CV is a comprehensive document and a résumé can be tailored from the former according to the requirement of a job. For the sake of convenience of designing, both the documents can be divided into three major parts—the opening, the middle and the closing. The following table highlights their formats, segments and techniques of writing in a comparative form:

a. The Beginning

A Comparison between a résumé and a CV

Headings	Résumé	CV
1. Headline	Begins with a headline giving: Name, address, e-mail ID, Tel, no., and fax no	Not given
2. Desired Position	Stated	Not given
3. Career Objective	One sentence—statement of career goals—job specific and not vague, need not be in high-fl own English, communicates self-motivation and interest (specimen is given after the table)	Not given
4. Personal Details	Comes in the closing part (see below)	• Begins with personal details: Name (capital letters), address, Tel. no., e-mail ID, fax, nationality, date of birth, marital status • All entries are listed one below the other

Some specimen of career objectives

i. To work on a suitable position in a prestigious Electrical Component Production Set-up, where I can learn with experience, utilize my existing skills and grow in my relevant field, contributing to the development of the organization. (This type of objective will be more suitable for fresh candidates.)

ii. To contribute to the growth of a prominent company by seeking a managerial opening in the recruitment division of HR department and thus explore new HR skills for such senior posts (appropriate for a senior and experienced person).

Headings	Résumé	CV
1. Work Experience	Only relevant work experience	Complete work experience
2. Education	Relevant qualifications, trainings, etc., are mentioned. (Highlight your educational details if you are a new job applicant.)	• Qualifications, degrees, training, schooling, names of institutions/university, years of passing, grades/division. • Seminars/workshops attended, research projects undertaken and publications, etc., may be given under separate headings.

(Continued)

3. Skills and Personality Traits	Only special skills suitable to the targeted position are listed, for example, expertise in a related computer language/data processing/knowledge of foreign languages/interpersonal skills/ leadership qualities	May be listed but more broadly
4. Achievements	Only concerned achievements are listed or those that differentiate you from others and show that you are a go-getter and can take challenges	Distinctions, awards, merits, scholarships, fellowships, a prestigious research project, or anything that conveys recognition.

b. The Middle: This is the functional segment of your document and should be designed very carefully as the major part of your interview deals with the data given here.

Employers are interested in your work experience, professional skills and achievements as such things give you an edge over the others. Support such information with relevant documents and facts.

c. The Closing:

Headings	*Résumé*	*CV*
1. Activities and Interests	Extra/co-curricular activities/hobbies, memberships, participation in sports, seminars, exhibitions, quizzes, academic and cultural competitions (only special items briefly and in points)	• Little elaborated but in composite form • These things show that you are a multifaceted and dynamic personality
2. Personal	A résumé closes with personal details—age, nationality, driving license and passport no., married/unmarried*; children* (* optional)	A CV opens with personal details (see above).
3. References	2–3 names of referees (holding a responsible position) who can recommend your name for the concerned post. Names, designations, addresses, and telephone nos. should be given.	Same as in a résumé